HOME HEALTH

MARKETING

BIBLE

———————————————————————————

HOME HEALTH

MARKETING

BIBLE

The 4-Dimensional Approach

Maxim A. Azarov

Home Health Marketing Bible: The 4-Dimensional Approach

ISBN-13: 978-0-9820924-3-9 (hardcover)
ISBN-10: 0-9820924-3-1 (hardcover)

Printed in the United States of America

To Talitha, my beautiful soulmate.

Thank you for inspiring me.

I am so proud of you.

CONTENTS

Introduction

EVERY OTHER SALES SEMINAR I HAVE EVER attended teaches what has become a cliché of each and every single sales book of marketing ABCs: "Always Be Closing!" If you are in Home Health sales and you believe that "Always Be Closing" attitude will get you referrals – keep reading, you are in for a big surprise. This book has a lot of ABCs but this paragraph is the first and the last one where you will read that particular one. Rather, we will start with the most important ABC in Home Health:

> ## Always Be Cautious

Being cautious in Home Health business is everything. Being cautious can mean a difference between your sales failing miserably or succeeding beyond your imagination. Be cautious when choosing who you deal with, how you deal with them and, most importantly, whose advice you take when it comes to sales and marketing.

Home Health industry has been a part of American industry for decades and yet professionally guided training and sales approach are still noticeably absent in Home Health marketing today. Throughout the recent years, marketing to physicians has slowly graduated from the old "trial and error" approach to a tried and true, applied science, presented in this book from a very distinct perspective of a Home Health Agency.

In recent years, there has been an explosion of new "home-baked" seminars, sales books and websites on Home Health Marketing by so-called "experts". Majority of them are presented by either failed business owners, perpetual "sales coaches" or important-title, low-value consultants, making a career out of awkwardly applying old car sales tricks to a very intricate healthcare marketing. All are oddly detached from any sort of day-to-day, real world Home Health sales and marketing techniques. No matter how many attendees those "home-baked" seminars gather, be cautious, the only recipe they provide is the one for a certain sales disaster.

Being cautious is, indeed, everything. Spend your time and your money wisely. Here are the common red flags of seminars and books that will steal both, providing no return for your hard-earned money:

- Their curriculum vitae on the back of the book or a seminar description strangely excludes any kind of relevant university degree.

- Their prior job titles are vague and there is no specific mention of any company they worked for with the exception of the one that is selling you the seminar or the book.

- They claim to have been coaching Home Health clients for decades without being directly involved in Home Health sales process.

- After reading their books and attending their seminars, you are left with the feeling, "man, it looks like I've been cheated again", and, trust me, you most likely have been.

As the author of this book, I feel it is important to mention at least some of my credentials in this introduction.

Upon coming from Moscow, Russia to the United States, I've graduated with a Bachelor of Arts Degree in Communications with emphasis in Economics from DePauw University. Throughout the years, I have had the honor to work for Eli Lilly Pharmaceuticals in Indianapolis, Indiana as a part of the marketing team launching Actos® for Type II diabetes in the U.S.

Additionally, I worked with Eli Lilly's Global Team as a part of the Competitive Intelligence Project. In 2002, I was hired and received training as a part of the professional pharmaceutical sales team working with Boehringer-Ingelheim Pharmaceuticals and responsible for marketing of Flomax® and other medications in the Great Lakes Region.

I was introduced to Home Health industry after being hired by Dyna Care Home Health, one of the nation's largest Home Health agencies, which was eventually bought out by Amedisys (NasdaqGS: AMED).

Presently, I am honored to work on several marketing, strategy development and direct sales projects for a number of high volume, fast growing home health care agencies in Chicago, as well as growing my own marketing/consulting business.

Now that the cautions and introductions are out of the way, it's time to learn how this book can bring you truly great quality sales, right business relationships and much, much more!

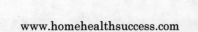

PART 1

Laying The Groundwork

Chapter 1

Getting Your Doctor's Referral Pad

(Legally)

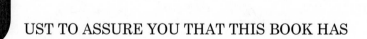

JUST TO ASSURE YOU THAT THIS BOOK HAS

not been written to fill the pages with typical sales seminar
nonsense material, we dedicate this chapter to a very
common issue for many sales people working in home
health industry, which is... not owning your physician's
referral pad and how to be in charge of one when it comes to
your referrals. This goes hand-in-hand with the second ABC
you will need to know before you proceed with the rest of
this book.

Always **B**e **C**onsulting

A little illustration first. Back when one of my companies was undergoing a certain amount of non-marketing related issues, I felt that in order to get us back on track, we needed a fresh look on how our company operated. Being an Always-Be-Cautions type of a guy, I have been very careful when we have finally hired one outstanding individual to work as our company's consultant.

Normally, it takes an extraordinary amount of effort for any person to get on my "trustworthy" list because I know that people are often driven by greed and self-promotion, expecting a big pay for a very abstract pie-in-the-sky return on investment, and yet, our new consultant proved again and again and again that her idea of work consisted of bringing our company *VALUE* first. Her work ethic and value-first-pay-later approach made our company fully depend on her advice, her feedback and her subtle suggestions on workflow improvement.

As her consultative role in our company grew, gradually almost ALL of the decisions had to be verbally approved by her before coming to fruition. The decisions she influenced ranged from hiring and firing employees to the kinds of software and supplies we used in the company. When a sales person would come in to see the company's owner, on many occasions, the decision to use or not use a certain service had to be relayed through her first.

I can imagine, at this point in the chapter, about half of the people already know where this illustration is going, while the other half feels helplessly lost, asking "How can all this help me in owning my doctor's referral pad?"

Any more or less successful business, be it a home health agency, a physician's practice or a clinic, almost always has a highly respected consultant/mentor position whose opinion matters and whose opinions are not likely to be overridden. Those are the people of trust and influence and they have the ability to drastically change the flow of the company's operations without actually having any management or any ownership ties to the company.

For you to "own" your physician's or case manager's referral pad, you will have to forget the word "salesman" and replace it with the word "Referral Consultant" whenever referring to yourself. Being a "consultant" will give you powers to completely change, move, operate and change the referral flow patterns of those you "consult." Everyone can be a good or a bad sales person, yet only those who will take on the position of a trustworthy consultant will be able to dramatically tip the scale of referral flow, whether they come from a physician's office or a hospital.

If you already know what it takes to transform yourself from a sales person to a Referral Consultant, you can go ahead and skip down to the last page of this book because I think it is important that you at least read credits at the end. If you do not feel like you are quite there yet, this book is written to talk about WHAT IT TAKES to be a Referral Consultant as well as the HOW-TO or the practical approach of getting to be a Referral Consultant or a Sales Sapiens, a new breed of sales people on the market today.

Here are the 8 factors that mold a Professional Referral Consultant:

1.   **Trust Factor**

2.   **Helping Mind/Helping Hand Factor**

3.   **Consistency /Availability Factor**

4.   Reliability Factor

5.   Product Knowledge Factor

6.   Leading the Process and Setting the Guidelines
       Factor

7.   Going the Extra Mile Factor

1. Trust Factor.

Trust Factor has to do with never, under any
circumstances, giving information that is inaccurate,
misleading, straight-out false or one-sidedly self-serving.
Trust is the foundation of your consulting relationship with
the doctor or a case manager if you are ever going to have
one. One misstep will cause you to lose your referral source
and possibly damage your reputation forever.

For instance, never say your home health agency has an in-
house electrical stimulation equipment if you don't have one
or if you normally outsource it. Never say that your nurses
commonly go to remote areas if you do not know if they
would actually go there. Never promise anything or assume
anything until you know the answer for sure. If you say
that you will take a Medicaid patient, then, certain is the

day, when you will get one and for better or worse you will absolutely have to take one. This is because if you don't, you will ruin the foundation of a possibly great business relationship forever.

Never assume anything. During one of my in-services in one of the largest hospitals in Chicago, I opened a floor for any questions about our agency. "Do you have Physical Therapists?" someone asked and I said, "Absolutely!"; "Do you do IV infusion?" someone asked and I said, "You bet!". Then a cardiology case manager in the back asked "What about Radio…" she proceeded to describe a kind of a treatment I have never heard about. A salesman in me wanted to shout out, "Of course! We do it every day!" However, I have decided to not assume anything. "I have never heard about it," I said. "But maybe if you can write it down for me, I will ask someone in the office," I added and began to pass a sheet of paper and a pen to the asking case manager. She said she didn't need any paper and laughed. She admitted that it was a trick question to weed out sales people who say "yes" to absolutely everything they ask them.

Trust is everything. The day you lose trust, you lose your referral source forever.

2. Helping Mind / Helping Hand Factor.

It is beyond the "small talk", "how are your kids" and basketball game tickets. The Helping Mind Factor has to do with your ability to effectively share your objective, valuable opinion, whether the issue you asked about is or isn't related to your services.

Here's an example. When asked about any subject matter, strive to contribute with your sincere, non-self-serving recommendations.

Serve as a helping mind in a doctor's practice.

Help the doctor's patients. If one of the patients does not have Medicare – arrange a social worker visit for them in an attempt to help, even if it does not lead to a referral. If one of the doctor's patients needs a cane – suggest a place where to get it, even if it is not associated with your company.

Be helpful in things other than referrals. If a case manager or a physician begins to attentively ask you about a certain patient case or, maybe, some unrelated new business ventures, or his plans to expand, feel free to encourage, support, give positive, constructive, non-self-serving suggestions. Once you establish yourself as a trustworthy companion who gives valuable and honest feedback, whose opinion matters, you will be well on your way to firmly establishing yourself in a position of a Professional Referral Consultant.

Help in other ways. By the way, in my sales experience, I have not only been used as a helping mind, but, often, as a helping hand as well. One of the physicians I knew would always ask me to help him carry a pretty heavy portable EKG machine from his office in the hospital to his vehicle. Typically on the following day, he would always give me all of his discharged referrals for that week.

3. Consistency / Availability Factor.

Just like you would never buy a chair that holds you only fifty percent of the time, you will not see a referral for as long as a physician or a case manager does not see you as a consistent Referral Consultant.

Consistency and Availability are also closely associated with one other factor on the list – Reliability.

You have to be consistent in your follow-ups, showing your face in doctor's office, in your punctuality, in your professionalism and in your responsiveness to arising issues. If you have been bringing one lunch a month to a physician's office for 3 months and then no lunches for the next six – you will end up being seen as either unavailable or unreliable, although it may not be true about you at all.

Whatever your routing schedule is, follow it. If your routing schedule shows you to visit a certain doctor every other Thursday, at 10am, then show up there, without exceptions, every other Thursday at 10am.

From experience, inconsistency in follow-ups can lead to a variety of damaging situations. Office staff may forget your name, or the company you work with, or the services that you offer. In one instance, when I stopped showing up at one of the doctor's office for more than six months, one of the people working in the office simply assumed that I must have changed companies and stopped sending referrals. Moreover, the same office person shared her assumptions with the rest of the medical "crew", spreading the news, gradually from office to office, from floor to floor, until even the Director of Case Management of the hospital assumed that I have "abandoned" them.

Here is another damaging effect of inconsistency. Imagine that your home health agency provides approximately the same kind and quality of service as your competitor who gets all the business for one reason or another. Occasionally, sales opportunity for you, as an agency becomes a sort of a waiting game. Another home health agency, inevitably, given enough time, is bound to mess up. After a number of those mess-ups, a frustrated physician or a case manager is bound to call the next person down the list, and, if you are easily available and consistent with your follow ups, that person will be you.

Probably one of the easiest sales jobs I have ever held was working as a sales person for a laboratory. Any laboratory, medium or large, handles hundreds and hundreds of specimens on a monthly basis. Competitor's mess-ups were virtually inevitable, be it a small or a big laboratory.

This meant that my job as a sales rep was easily reduced to merely showing up consistently, a few times a month in every target physician's office, and telling them that if they try us, there was no way in the world the mess ups would occur. This somewhat re-active strategy allowed me to sell our services to one physician after the other for as long as I worked for that particular laboratory.

Home health services are somewhat similar to laboratory services in a way that given enough time, one of the competitor's patients will complain, or see worsening of the symptoms, or will grow tired of a nurse not showing up on time. This means that every single time you would show up on the physician's office doorstep, his mind will continue to wonder: "What if? What if I gave that agency a try? Maybe, just maybe, all of my headaches will go away."

And one of these days, tired of dealing with other home health agency's issues, your target doctor's "What if?" will turn into "I've had enough! I need to switch to a different home health agency today!"

This would be the time (provided you have been consistently available) to give the doctor your business card and tell him to dial your agency's referral hotline.

There is another important moment of the availability factor. If you are always available, the physician or a case manager will mentally associate your availability as a Sales Consultant with your company's availability when it comes to treating patients.

Have you ever tried to sign up for something over the phone? Have you ever been so incredibly enthusiastic dialing the phone number... only to hear a pre-recorded message saying something like, "The next available sales representative will be with you in (voice changes) eighteen (voice changes again) minutes." Somehow, I seem to have that experience almost every time I try to call and sign up for something over the phone, including the time when I was eager to have the website for my seminars built by a well-advertised web design company. Incredibly, it took me at least 20 minutes before I was able to talk to an available sales person.

You know the two things that come to my mind when I hear about any kind of a wait when I am standing on the other end of the phone line, holding a credit card in my hand waiting to pay? Number one is, that they simply do not care about my business. Number two is, that if it is going to take this long to buy their service, how long of a wait is it going to take me when any kinds of issues arise?

Interestingly enough, physicians and case managers alike tend to correlate your sales process with the service of your company. Are you consistent? Responsible? Available? Then, they begin to believe, your company can be trusted. And this leads us to another factor that will help you to be virtually in charge of your physician's referral pad: Reliability Factor.

4. Reliability Factor.

Aside from my sales experiences in the medical field, I have learned some of my most valuable lessons from owning my first graphic design/marketing business from a seemingly completely different industry – funeral home industry. As I have developed relationships with dozens of funeral home directors in our area, I offered them a very unique product, complete personalization of each individual funeral service they have ever held, from specialty service programs, to memorial DVD memorabilia, to custom design casket panels that completely transformed a normally dry-looking funeral arrangement. Many of the funeral home directors commented that many of their clients would choose their funeral home over others simply because they had the very unique, personalized service my company provided for them.

Unlike any other business I've ever been a part of, timing was the key issue with this one. If the funeral is scheduled for 11am, two days from now, I am at the mercy of that specific time. Else, I may as well scratch off that particular funeral home off my list of customers. If it was going to mean staying up a night or two without sleep, it had to be done. No matter what. I've gained my customers loyalty and exclusivity to the point where even large-chain funeral conglomerate affiliates would call me asking to combine our services.

I have built my business on quality and reliability, and when the time came to move on, my customers had nothing but good things to say about the business I have built.

Reliability has to do with being dependable. Once the medical office you are calling on is used to your presence, knows that you are readily available, consistent and trustworthy individual who will go out of his way to help them, or a patient, you will be the only one getting the referrals.

Reliability has also a lot to do with delivering on your promises, no matter how small or big. Often, a new home health sales representative sees him/herself as someone who depends on a doctor for their existence. Remember, being dependent on your doctor for your existence will not get you to the top of the home health game. Make your goal to have your doctor depend on you and only then you will come out on top!

5. Product Knowledge Factor
(Or how to become "the other Case Manager")

Product knowledge and product presentation are so vital to your role of being a Professional Referral Consultant that both are described in much more detail in the section of this book that deals with Communication.

Here is what the real deal is. This world is inundated with sales people with their meaningless sales pitches, but the true specialists of their trade, those people who know every single aspect and angle of their product, are hard to find, and those are the ones that really matter in any business. Often people are willing to put up with many issues just to know that they are working with a professional.

Be "the other Case Manager" for your physician or a hospital! Know your product well enough for a medical staff to completely count on you whether it's a simple or a difficult case. Most of the hospitals have a Director of Case Management position. Be their helping mind as well as their helping hand! Know your product well enough to recommend them, objectively, what to do with a certain case and if the advice you give them works for them once, they will use you over and over again.

If you feel like you have been "thrown" into the home health sales position with very little or virtually no training – you are not alone. Countless agencies hire sales people coming from a variety of backgrounds literally hoping that out of those they hire, some will go on to become great home health salespeople, while the bad ones will eventually leave on their own or get fired. Home health industry is well known for substandard HR practices and undertraining its sales force. Most sales people start going out on the field, by themselves, within the first two days of being hired.

It is no secret that doctors often are much more receptive to seeing pharmaceutical sales representatives than home health sales coordinators. One of the reasons is the fact that home health representatives are often (and sometimes deservingly so) expected to offer very little educational or any other value to a doctor.

Additionally, unlike pharmaceutical representative jobs that commonly require a Bachelor's Degree (MBA preferred) with GPA of 3.2 or above, plus a minimum of 2 years of prior pharmaceutical sales experience and no more than 2 job changes within the last several years, physicians know that when it comes to hiring a sales representative by a home health agency, there are simply no industry standards.

This is just another reason why a typical physician does not appreciate his time wasted on someone who does not know his or her "stuff". As a result, they tend to limit their time with agency representatives. According to one doctor, she has seen dozens of home health sales reps with or without a university degree talking about how "caring" their agency is. However, there is one kind of home health sales rep she doesn't see too often: a knowledgeable one.

Unlike my first home health sales assignment, my pharmaceutical sales contract clearly stated that my employment with the company was at all times conditional on my product knowledge grading. Scoring below 90% on product knowledge tests, as well as sales skill tests meant automatic termination.

Like no other job I've had before, I have spent my first 3 weeks with the pharmaceutical company studying ridiculously thick educational binders of human anatomy, physiology and sales skills. The studying was done on my own as well as with the product knowledge advisor. With his approval, I was given permission and a ticket to fly out of state to test my written and my verbal understanding of products and company's sales techniques. Scoring over 90% qualified me to receive a much more in-depth training at the company's headquarters (also out of state). After two more weeks of training, I was finally eligible to take exams on everything I have learned up until that point. When by that point I thought that my education as a pharmaceutical sales representative was over, I have learned that I was deeply mistaken.

It was only after I came back, I have realized that I was going to have yet another 6 months of on-the-field training

before returning to headquarters to take more advanced
product knowledge exams.

It would be safe to assume that no home health agency
known to me provides this kind of training system to its
employees. This means that product knowledge and sales
skill development are things you may have to do on your
own. Even if you spend some 10-30 minutes each day with
the senior sales representative, or on the internet, learning
the details of home health operations and how it can benefit
physicians, you will be that much better equipped when
talking and advising your referral sources.

A physician with an extremely difficult orthopedic case,
who normally may be "encouraged" by the hospital to use
only their own hospital-affiliated agency, most of the time
will go out of his way to refer the case to a representative
that knows, sells and helps coordinate difficult orthopedic
cases. This has been proven true again and again in my
own professional sales experience.

Being a pro at knowing your product and your market will
be your trump card when dealing with both, your target

market, such as your physician or a case manager, as well as your employer. If you are someone who knows the product, the field, the industry and its insides and outs, your employers would pay for your skills, whether you are in sales, marketing or in any other field of your home health agency.

Knowing your product is truly a great asset to have. For a number of years, one of the home health agencies I know has been working with an attorney charging what sometimes added up to be thousands of dollars for a few hours of work and yet they consistently chose him exclusively to work on whatever legal issues that came up in their company. The reason was not because he had a word "Attorney" in front of his name on the business card. It was the fact that he was capable in handling every possible case that would be given to him and turn it into a win-win situation.

In today's world, the new currency on the market is your *KNOWLEDGE*, not your *TITLE*. In home health industry, people who get paid the most (and on occasion more than people running the company) are the professionals who could care less about what their business card says. They are the sales people, the nurses and the consultants that "know their stuff" inside and out.

If you are new to the home health industry, learn how to become a sponge that survives by taking in everything in its surroundings, yet absorbing only what's needed. Read books (but be cautious what books you read), go sell, make mistakes, learn, sell again, and most importantly, listen to the ones that have done it before.

I cannot tell you how many times I had to deal with someone coming from a completely different sales field, defiant to the advice of the experienced and attempting to do things that have been proven not to work.

The bottom line here is this. Know your product, present it well, never make statements that you do not know for a fact to be true and you will be amazed by the results to follow.

6. Leading The Process And Setting The Guidelines Factor.

(or why the customer is not always right)

Here is the biggest sales paradox. Any kind of sales training will tell you the customer is always right. Right?

Not necessarily. In fact, much of the time, customers are dead wrong and it is how we deal with them being wrong is what sets successful businesses apart from the unsuccessful ones.

The customer (or the physician or a case manager in this instance) will never know the details of your business as well as you do. They do not know the industry's ins and outs, they do not know prices, reimbursements, the intricate details of Medicare payments. The customers do not know a lot of things. Your goal as a Professional Referral Consultant during each visit is to educate them on how you can help them by leading them through the process, explaining to them how your company works and what can and cannot be done. In a paradoxical way, the customers tend to stay with those companies that lead, guide and direct them as opposed to those who are willing to change their standards at the slight whisper of their words.

Do we need to listen to customers? Absolutely. Even when they do not know what they are talking about? Of course! The only thing you are not allowed to do is to allow your customer to lead you as a sales person. If you allow your customers to lead you, they will lead you right out of sales, whether you are selling retail or a medical service. Here is a more specific example.

Back in the days when I was still actively hands-on with my design business, while talking to one of the business clients of mine, he admitted to me that he was so impressed with my design work that he wanted me to make more catalogs of my products to give out to each and every customer of his business. Needless to say, I was very happy about that.

"The only thing," he added, "I really like your designs that have a picture of a dove, blended into the background," he continued. "In fact, I would really love it if you could re-make ALL OF YOUR CATALOGS, so that all of your designs had a big white dove on them," he smiled. "I think it will be a great opportunity for your business..." he added.

"If you change the catalogs, I am going to start buying much more from you, and so will your other customers!"

He was my business client, I thought, and that meant I must listen and do what he said, I convinced myself. Back then, I did not know how to lead the client and, hence, I followed my client's lead instead. The sales from my original catalogs were great, and all I had to do was to convince my business client to use the original catalogs, as it was the part of the process that I have established. And yet, I did not follow my instincts.

I knew that the doves on my designs, while loved by some people, were not much appreciated by others. This was the exact reason I left them out from my catalogs before. Nevertheless, in order to impress my business client, I've interrupted my workflow and have spent countless hours, nights and days, remaking my catalogs of designs until every single one of them had a dove picture on them. Being a small business, I took the little money I had and invested them in printing those catalogs. Within only a couple of weeks, I have given my new catalogs to the guy who requested the "dove" change. He also convinced me to give

out the rest of the catalogs to my other business clients.
And here is when I've learned a big lesson.

The requests for my designs altogether went down
drastically. As business owners presented my catalogs to
their retail customers, they did not seem to be as excited
about them and I could not figure out why.

In a perfect world, any feedback would be immediate.
However in real world, if you make a mistake, sometimes it
may take you months before you know if you did. The
customers did not like the doves. However, they did not
want to hurt my business client's feelings by saying
anything about my doves, and my business clients did not
want to hurt mine. Finally, after at least 3 months of me
giving out my new "dove" catalogs, I slowly began receiving
comments from customers who did not like the fact that
doves were on every single template I had. As a result, my
sales went down. It was only when I printed an old version
of the catalog with the doves on only some of the pages, did
my sales gradually start climbing back up, but not before
I've suffered a major business setback. I was led off my

established process, I did not follow my business knowledge and I paid for the lesson big time!

What I have learned from the ordeal was that you got to be the one that has the ultimate knowledge of your product and your industry. You ARE the Professional Sales Consultant for your home health agency! Not anyone else! You know and you are the one in the best position to find out what works for your specific type of business and what doesn't. Lead the process step by step and do not allow anyone to lead you! Be a firm (although not stubborn), trustworthy consultant for a physician or a case manager!

I can pretty much guarantee that as a home health marketing representative, you WILL be pushed around by at least some of the potential referral sources with all kinds of crazy ideas and suggestions. Do not fall for it! Instead, lead them through the sales process that is already established and is proven to work!

Do not allow medical office staff to lead you around their finger with worthless referrals, counterproductive ideas and endless meetings that will have no benefit to your mutual business, etcetera. "Oh, Mr.Representative, we will give you a referral as long as you sponsor this and this provided by our doctor. This would be a great opportunity..." What a load of nonsense! "Miss Office Manager, I am sorry, we would love to sponsor so and so, however this is not a part of our process. My manager is not likely to approve it if he does not see at least one referral from your office before we sponsor anything."

This approach may seem counter-intuitive, but in real life, this approach is the only one that works. While still learning the home health ropes as a sales rep for another company, I have witnessed my manager accepting three Medicaid patients from a hospital in hopes that, one of these days, he will get a paying Medicare referral from them, in spite of the fact that it was not a part of the company's established process. "It will be a great opportunity..." a discharge planner kept explaining to my manager "to show what your agency can do for us and I promise to give you your Medicare referral as soon as I have one."

Just another fairy tale! I could not believe my manager fell for it. He's been pushed around with referrals that were never going to be even submitted for billing and, sure enough, after the last one, the discharge planner from that particular hospital stopped answering phone calls from my manager altogether. Surprise? Not really.

When your selling begins to turn into some kind of a give-and-take child's playground, it is time to remember that there is only one position you, as an effective Professional Referral Consultant can take – and it is the position of a playground's supervisor. In this position, you will have to get control of your sales process and tell your potential referral sources that there are certain processes you need to follow and their requests are simply not a part of it. Trust me, it will be ok.

Lead your physicians, discharge planner, or case managers through the process. Do not allow yourself to ever be manipulated for the sake of the sale, or you will definitely lose one. Educate your physicians on what your home health agency represents, NOT how much pushing around you can take just to get a referral.

Establish your agency in the eyes of the physician as the one with the solid reputation, specific guidelines and knowledge of the product. If you accept only Medicare, say it straight up and say it right away.

Also, do not build up expectations you can't uphold. Do not mislead anyone and it will prevent you from being misled. Wrong input, as we all know it, leads to wrong output and, ultimately, lousy sales results.

We do not go to McDonalds asking if we could have crab sushi instead of fries. McDonalds has an exceptional service and they do a lot of extraordinary things to keep their multi-billion customer base coming back, but making crab sushi is simply not one of them. They have successfully educated the customer that neither begging nor complaining will change their menu and we've all learned to live with it and still go there for whenever we want food made fast.

The process approach, additionally, has its foundation in the modern psychology. All of us, no matter how strong and independent, want to be led. In the back of our minds, we always need someone, physical or metaphysical to rely on, someone to depend on, someone to lean on. Being a knowledgeable Professional Referral Consultant with a very well developed sales approach allows you to be the person representing the agency that can be leaned on when times are tough.

At this point of this book, I can already see a number of experienced sales representatives with the Customer-Always-Right approach who would do anything for their client, shaking their head in disbelief. On the contrary, they would say, we should do everything we can for our customers no matter what! This indicates that they have just completely missed the point of drawing a clear line between leading the sale and allowing others to lead you right out of their office.

Of course this is not to say that going the extra mile cannot be a part of your Professional Referral Consultant sales approach.

7. Going the Extra Mile Factor

Going The Extra Mile Factor is the key to repeat referrals and the referrals that are a direct result of a word of mouth advertisement. One of the most valuable lessons about customer service, was the one I received at one of my first jobs out of college working for one of the largest car rental agencies in the United States. One of the criteria for promotion within the company was customer satisfaction index for each individual branch. This was monitored by randomly placing phone calls to recent customers asking them to describe their prior experiences of renting a car. Only a "completely satisfied" answer counted. The branch where I started working at, had the lowest customer satisfaction in the entire region with only around a half of all the customers satisfied with our services. That meant that every meeting our branch manager kept on us to do whatever it takes to make sure that our customers were coming back to us. And, oh, boy, we did.

If a customer wanted a very specific pick-up location, we did it. If a customer wanted a mid-size car, we would throw in a free upgrade at no cost. We would serve them soda while they were waiting in line, drive them back to their house if they have forgotten their credit card or their driver's license.

On one occasion, one of my customers, without probably even realizing it, gave me an expired driver's license. Fearing that by the time her license was going to be renewed she might go to a competitor company, I drove her to the local Bureau of Motor Vehicles, waited about an hour in line until she had her license renewed and drove her back to our branch where she could, finally, legally rent a car. Customer service was everything! While wearing suits and ties we would clean and vacuum our cars spotless until there was not a dirty speck anywhere in sight. On many occasions, I was yelled at by my manager for wearing a tie that was practically falling apart at the bottom, as a result of being sucked into the car vacuum so many times. At the end of each rental, we would ask each customer if they were completely satisfied with our services, and if not, what we could have done to make their experience better.

Going the extra mile for any customer was in each and every one of us up until our customer satisfaction index went to the high 90s. Our customers were coming back to us for more rentals and our profits have soared.

Once, as I was picking up a customer from a residence, I got a little lost and ended up circling the area for what seemed to be at least a few minutes. "This is a proof", I told my customer, "that in our company, we go the extra mile for a customer, whether it is needed or not!" We both laughed.

Home health environment is quite different from rent-a-car environment and yet, most of the human factors of keeping a customer, whether it is your physician, a customer manager, or a patient, remain the same. If your manager does not track your customer satisfaction index and going the extra mile is an option at your agency, here are some pointers that will help you score big when it comes to keeping your referral sources loyal to you and only you.

From experience, the most effective way to score some "extra mile" points is by immediately following up on a referral that was faxed to you. Call back to the doctor's office to confirm that the referral is received and when the patient is going to be seen by the nurse. Once the nurse has seen the patient, make a call back to the doctor's or case manager's office and leave a message about the condition of the patient and/or the status of the referral. If a Physical Therapist was recommended, let them know when and who is going to see the patient.

Whether it is a case manager, a physician or a physician assistant working with the discharged patients, most of their time is spent following up on whatever happened to the patient. Often their frustration with other home health agencies, including their unresponsiveness, is the prime opportunity to impress the physician's medical office by going just a little further than others are willing to go.

If a patient does not have a way to pay for medications, refer them to a social worker, even though they might not be eligible for your home health services. You can always bring it up next time you are visiting a doctor to help position your home health agency as the one that goes the extra mile.

Once again, if the patient does not have Medicare, refer him or her to someone who can help them apply for the benefits.

If they are in dire need of a durable medical equipment device, help them by referring them to an appropriate DME company, even though they might not end up being your patient.

As I am writing this chapter, visiting patients is far from being even a remote part of my job. Nevertheless, when one of the agencies I work with needed someone who can translate from Russian, I was readily available to travel to a place of her residence, one hour away, because I know it can mean a lot to the agency's business in the future. And although the lady will not need home health services for probably more than one certification period, she was so happy that someone who knows Russian has visited her that she promised to tell all of her neighbors and her doctor great things about our company.

Going the extra mile is about caring for your patient, your doctor, your case manager and whoever may come in contact with your company in the future and believe me, every single step of that extra mile will come back to you tenfold.

If your home health agency does not have a practice of collecting satisfaction survey from your patients, talk to your manager and make one of your own. Your manager can require a satisfaction survey to be placed in every packet. Along with regular check boxes, a satisfaction survey must contain an attached sheet of paper where a patient can describe in detail the reasons he or she is happy or not happy with the service. Example of the satisfaction survey can be found at the end of this chapter.

There are a couple of reasons how this could help your sales. First, you would know which nurses and which therapists are associated with the greater satisfaction levels. And secondly, every positive comment will outweigh the glossiest brochure or sales piece your agency could ever come up with. Keep all the positive comments in your sales folder and feel free to show them not only to the doctor or the case manager who referred you the patient, but to other referral sources as well. Unlike OBQI scores published by Medicare, the real-life comments in your folder will carry a lot more information for anybody who will be choosing to do business with your company.

HOME HEALTH SATISFACTION QUESTIONNARIE

Please rate the overall quality of care by placing a checkmark at the appropriate field where applicable:

	Poor	Good	Excellent
Registered Nurse			
Licensed Practical Nurse			
Certified Nurse Assistant			
Physical Therapist			
Occupational Therapist			
Social Worker			
Other			

	Yes	No
Staff arrives as planned		
The staff can be reached when needed		
Staff treated me with respect		
Staff let me participate in making care plans		
Staff explained to me my rights, advance directives and procedures related to my care		
The office staff was courteous and helpful		
I would recommend this agency to my friends and relatives		

NOTES:

Chapter 2

Home Health Marketing:

4-Dimensional Approach Overview

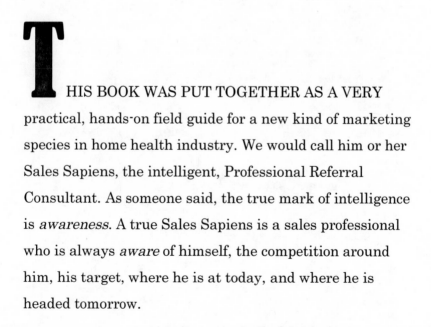

THIS BOOK WAS PUT TOGETHER AS A VERY practical, hands-on field guide for a new kind of marketing species in home health industry. We would call him or her Sales Sapiens, the intelligent, Professional Referral Consultant. As someone said, the true mark of intelligence is *awareness*. A true Sales Sapiens is a sales professional who is always *aware* of himself, the competition around him, his target, where he is at today, and where he is headed tomorrow.

In the old days, the most widespread sales model was a Point-Of-Sale, a one-dimensional model focusing directly on how to present yourself and what to do when talking directly to your customer in order to *close the sale*. This book will go into detail on a few crucial aspects of the Point-Of-Sale approach, as a part of a much larger sales process in direct relation to home health marketing, focusing on techniques and tools related to Preparation, Presence and Presentation (Figure 2.1).

The Point-Of-Sale approach, however, is only a small part of a much larger marketing picture. Quite some time ago, healthcare related industries began to realize that closing the sale is simply not enough, as it does not provide for developing relationship with your client over time. Sales, it appeared, was not a one time shot, but rather, a process. As a result, a two-dimensional model took the main stage of healthcare marketing, realizing the need for a Sales *Cycle* in contrast to the concept of Sales *Point* (Figure 2.2).

Figure 2.1 Point-Of-Sale Marketing

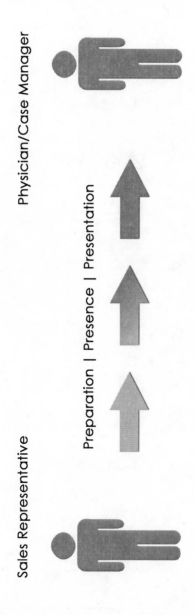

Figure 2.2 Sales Cycle Marketing

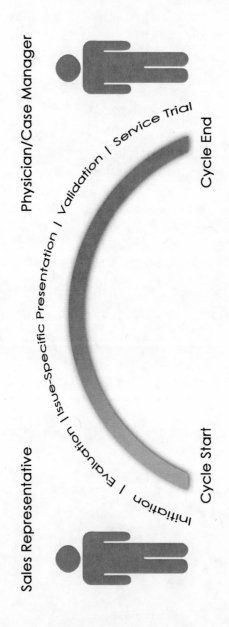

The Sales Cycle Concept, described in later chapters, allowed for a several- stage process leading from initial introduction to developing a strong bond between a sales person, physician and the product or service.

This book, however, goes many steps beyond the traditional, two-dimensional Sales Cycle by introducing the Sales Oxygenation Concept, where sales energy between the physician,the sales person, and the product, is being constantly replenished, similar to how oxygen is also constanly being replenished in the human arteries. If followed, this concept will secure the trust and loyalty of your referral sources, thereby generating for you a consistent flow of referrals from them(Figure 2.3).

Figure 2.3 Sales-Oxygenation Marketing

The fourth dimension, namely the Spheres of Influence is the most advanced level described in this book, exploring the effects of influence coming from seemingly unrelated sources in order to tremendously propel your sales level by allocating sufficient amount of time in order to explore what is commonly overlooked in a typical sales process (Figure 2.4).

This fourth dimension, in a way, provides the leverage necessary to play the sales game on a level with the other big guys of the industry, with the limited resources available in a mid-size, market-conscious home health agency, staffed with a high energy and unlimited motivation Sales Sapiens marketing team.

Figure 2.4 Spheres of Influence

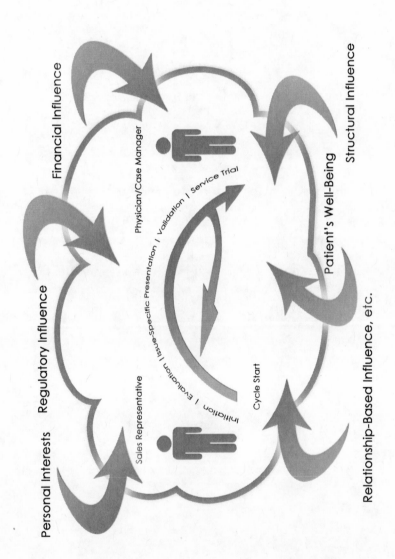

NOTES:

_____

_____

_____

_____

_____

_____

_____

_____

_____

_____

PART 2

First Dimenstion of Home Health Marketing

Chapter 3

First Dimension:

Preparation of Sales Sapiens

Or What I Have Learned From

Pharmaceutical Sales

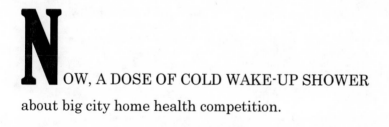

NOW, A DOSE OF COLD WAKE-UP SHOWER
about big city home health competition.

Medicare.gov provides a listing of over 150 agencies serving
the zip code where our agency is located. That means that if
you are looking for a Burger King in our local yellow pages,
you are more likely to find a newly opened Burger King
Home Health than your well-known burger joint. Only
joking, of course.

There are about a dozen of well-established hospitals in the area that send their business to home health agencies located in our county and in adjacent counties. Assuming that 150 agencies is a little excessive for a typical zip code, we will entertain the idea that there are about 300 total agencies we are trying to compete with in our market. With an average sales force of 7 sales people per agency, what does this all mean for our super extraordinary Sales Sapiens? And most importantly, what does this all mean for a hypothetical Dr.Hearditall and his typical day? Here it is.

Dr.Hearditall has at least 5 out of 2100 available home health representatives stopping by, introducing themselves and telling Dr.Hearditall something that goes like this: "Dr. Hearditall, I am Tok Tomuch with Tok Tomuch Home Health care, the Home Care that *Really Cares!*"

If at this point the rep was not already guided out of the door, then it goes like this. "We provide our patients with not only nurses, but PTs, OTs, STs, MSWs and we have the best staff and the best nurses and we go everywhere you want us to go! Here is a business card and a brochure, please keep us in mind, would you like some cookies that say *Tok Tomuch Home Health* on them?"

This is the point where the rep is guided to the rep food depository next to the secretary's desk consisting of cookies from Lord-Oh-Care Home Care, Starbucks delights from Care-To-Scare Home Care and Godiva chocolate from Care About Medicare Home Care (I made the names up, of course, and they do not represent actual home health agencies). The only difference is that now, the most prominent spot is taken by a cookie set from Tok Tomuch Home Care, because, after all, they are the home health agency (unlike those other imposters) that *really care* and (unlike those other imposters) should get a whole bunch of new referrals from the doctor!

Oh, Really?

Today, small to medium size home health agencies are on a prowl for time with the physician or hospital representatives as they compete with multi-billion pharmaceutical companies, multi-billion healthcare equipment companies and well-established home health agencies where nothing, absolutely nothing, is left to chance and any unprofessional remark, unprepared question, unethical objection, unprofessional appearance, and lousy presentation will leave your agency ponder, what in the world did we do wrong and why have we not seen any results yet?

This First Dimension of Home Health Marketing is here to help. We will start with Preparation of Sales Sapiens.

One of my big lessons from my pharmaceutical work had to do with… not coming to work. I will explain. I've always had a lot of enthusiasm for sales and was always eager to hit the road running. More running, I thought, meant more physician contacts, which, in turn meant more sales; one more "no" gets you one step closer to "yes"… Right?

Well kind of, except the "more running" part.

My pharmaceutical company's standard goal was to contact a minimum of 10 physicians a day. Not too bad. Only one day after the main part of my training was completed, in addition to getting a brand new company car (of my choosing) and an access to a storage full of drugs, I have received something I have never dreamed of – a physician database on a very nifty laptop. The fact that the database had many missing phone numbers, addresses, zip codes and hours of operation for the majority of the doctors, didn't bother me. It was more than I have ever expected to receive from any company and I was ready to make some major sales!!! I was expecting a day of colossal success and this is exactly why I could, in no way, expect the disaster that happened to me instead.

As I piled up my drug samples in the trunk of my slick and shiny Chevy Impala, I threw my new and nifty laptop on the passenger seat and headed to see my first "target doctor". After driving a route to his office that seemed to have taken me forever to get to, I, to my dismay, was greeted by a secretary who said that the doctor no longer worked there.

Yet, enthusiasm intact, I headed to see my second "target" only to find that he recently moved to a new, out of state location. My third "target" still worked in the same location, but somehow I failed to notice that he was a "target" for a totally different set of drugs from what I had in my car. Long story short, after driving for hours and standing in traffic through countless stoplights trying to visit one doctor after another, I saw a total of 2(!) doctors instead of 10. It turned out that some physicians have moved and others simply were not there due to their changed work schedule.

The high-tech approach of the pharmaceutical company I worked for required me to "synchronize" all of my contacts at the end of each day and, man, was it embarrassing when I had to synchronize mine. All of the members of my sales team could see my numbers, and, probably assumed that I just spent a whole day doing nothing! And, I might as well have!

To maintain my average visit per doctor on a 10 mark, I've decided to visit 18 doctors on the following day. Great idea?

Well, so it seemed until instead of 18, I, once again have visited only 2 more doctors after driving all day stumbling on the offices where the doc was absent, moved or was off on that day.

I had a bad feeling it was coming, and then it did. My manager, let's call him Doug, called me asking what was the problem and see if he could spend a day in the field with me. And when he did, he saw me going from one place to another, missing doctors, having a hard time finding the right drug samples or marketing materials in my car. After 3 unsuccessful attempts to see the doctors, he told me to pull over on the side of the road and told me... to take 3 days off work and gave me his corporate credit card. What???

I was in shock. First of all, 3 days off work will put me so far behind on my DVA (daily visit average) that I will never be able to catch up. And what was the deal with the credit card? It was then when Doug told me not to worry and spend the next 72 hours calling every single doctor in my database to update their place of work, hours of work, zip codes and the best day and time to visit them. And the card? I was allowed to spend up to $500 dollars on storage bins, containers and file folders to organize everything from drug samples, to marketing materials, to any possible documents in the trunk of my car by how often I use them and which ones are used together during a sales call to each doctor. Excited to have 3 days "off", I did precisely that. All of the doctors in my database could now be easily sorted by city, specialty, hours, and their best time to visit. The trunk of my car looked as pristine and organized as some neat-freak local pharmacy. I was ready to go and sell again. And so I have planned to visit another 10 doctors on the first day after my "break". The reality was, however, that the accurate database and my organized supplies allowed me to visit 15(!) in a single working day!

Preparation: Practical Approach

1. Software.

If you are still using paper to maintain your complete physician database – it is time to make an important addition. Get a professional database software! Get a laptop! Do not whine, cry and complain if your manager still did not give you one. Get one yourself! For software, if you work solo, I often suggest *QuickBooks Customer Manager*. If you are a part of a team marketing to the same organizations and physicians, I recommend *"ACT!"* by Sage as it can synchronize multiple visits by different representatives into one. Both types of software are very similar to the one that is currently being used by many multi-million dollar sales teams. Each software, though,

will have to be customized specifically to your preferences.
Our main website has some additional information on how
to group your target doctors and case managers by
physician group, location, day and time of visit and input
crucial information for an individual specialty of the office.
The hours you will spend learning the software will pay off
tenfold when you go out in the field. The use of professional
software will eliminate the need to plan your route for each
day of the week as you will be able to see your scheduled
list of calls simply with a few clicks of a mouse. Today, I
only use paper as an item of temporary convenience while
in the doctor's office before transferring the data into my
computer. You will read more about my use of paper later
in this book. However, if you still do not use computerized
databases you will be behind your competition the second
you leave your office to sell!

Both types of software I have mentioned can be easily
synchronized with Microsoft Outlook on your home
computer as a backup. This, in turn, will allow you to
synchronize all of your scheduled meetings and lunches
with your PDA or a phone organizer if you would like to do
so.

2. Sales Sapiens Preparation Phone Calls

Once you obtained and configured your software, it is time to put some information in, using the Preparation Sheet at the end of this chapter which is also available for download on our site (just in case you lose this book). Make as many copies as there are physicians you plan to visit.

Whether you are getting your referrals from an existing database or yellow pages, it is my recommendation to input at least 100 physicians to begin with, as a part of your bi-weekly doctor calls. This will allow for 80-100 physicians to be visited every 14 days, which is a perfect way to get yourself fully established in your territory before you start focusing on the accounts that have the highest potential.

The reason I prefer writing the initial pre-visit information on a Preparation Sheet first is that it will help you organize your questions when talking on the phone with the physician's secretary or a secretary in the hospital. It is important to ask if the physician uses home health services only if it is a new lead and to stay away from doctors of podiatry, optometrists, chiropractors and other physicians you may deem irrelevant for home health marketing.

Whenever you ask for a doctor's hours, normally, you don't want to spend more than 30 seconds on the phone. From experience, I found that most doctors do not hold the same hours every day and as a result, it is easier and faster to circle the days first and to write the time on lines below afterwards. For instance, when a receptionist says that doctor is available on Tuesdays and Wednesdays from 9 to 12, you will need to circle Tuesday and Wednesday on the first line of the Preparation Sheet and write down time below it. When the receptionist tells you that the doctor works from 3 to 5 on Fridays, circle Friday on the next line and write down 3 to 5 below it. This is truly a time-saving tool if you have ever called a physician's office to learn his or her hours of work. The usefulness will become apparent as you start calling to fill up your database with more and more new doctors.

Once all of your sheets are complete and transferred onto your computer database, you are now ready to move on to the next important element of your daily preparation: Sales Sapiens route mapping.

3. Sales Sapiens Route Mapping

Your daily route will become apparent once you sort your *Customer Manager database* or *ACT!* database by time and zip codes. However, finding the physician office is another question.

Everything has changed ever since navigation devices have entered our daily life. If you still do not have one, I suggest using mapquest to print out the maps of the physician offices' locations. Print out all of the offices' addresses from your daily route and place them in an accordion file, sorted out by each day of the week. This will greatly simplify your daily routing and mapping.

It is important to mention that the sales call preparation techniques described here are related only to getting ready for your very first visits. The Point-Of-Sale preparation is basic in nature and useful for sorting out medical offices based on their geographic location and the time of operation. Much more advanced preparation techniques related to targeting and evaluating specific doctors and individual sales strategies are described in sections dedicated to the other dimensions of home health sales.

Figure 3.1 Preparation Sheet

PHYSICIAN'S NAME _____

PHYSICIAN'S PHONE NUMBER _____

DOES THE PHYSICIAN USE HOME HEALTH
SERVICES? _____

OFFICE HOURS (Circle appropriate days and write the
appropriate time to visit)

M T W Th Fr Sat

   FROM _____ TO _____

M T W Th Fr Sat

   FROM _____ TO _____

M T W Th Fr Sat

   FROM _____ TO _____

M T W Th Fr Sat

   FROM _____ TO _____

M T W Th Fr Sat

   FROM _____ TO _____

NOTES:

_____

_____

_____

_____

_____

_____

_____

_____

_____

_____

Chapter 4

First Dimension: Presence

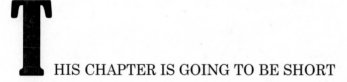

THIS CHAPTER IS GOING TO BE SHORT
and to the point, and yet, I already see a lot of sales people
for whom this chapter is nothing but a matter of common
sense. My experience, however, has proven over and over
that common sense is not given to everyone that gets hired
as a sales rep and often, a minute mistake in maintaining a
professional appearance can lead to disastrous results.

I remember, not too long ago, I spent hours preparing for one of our initial in-services with one of the top hospitals in the area. I prepared for what I hoped to be an impeccable presentation, showing the benefits of our home health agency over others in the area. I brought show-and-tell equipment and custom-assembled marketing packages for each one of the case managers that were going to be present.

I also planned to have one of our new sales representatives with me. I wanted her to be at the luncheon in order to show how we do presentations. On the day of the event, however, she was running a little late. I thanked everyone for coming and was about to start speaking. I was set for success!

However, what happened next turned out to be a disaster. Our new representative walked-in while unwrapping a chewing gum and within seconds placed it in her mouth… While chewing the gum so that everyone could see its bright blue color in her mouth, she thought it was going to be a great idea to start interrupting my presentation by saying "what he really meant to say was…" I could not believe my ears or my eyes. I could not believe it was happening to me. A lady who looked so professional during the interview process and training turned into a nightmare for my sales presentation.

But wait! There was more. She, apparently, have "prepared" for our presentation as well. She Xeroxed about a dozen black and white copies on a crumpled paper with font 36 letters that read one phrase: "If you have a referral, call me on my cell..." followed by her cell phone number in bold. I did not know where to hide.

I was so distracted by her appearance, her interruptions, and her home-made sheets of paper with her number on it, that I, as a presenter could no longer be focused on my presentation, and, I believe, neither could the nearly 12 case managers that came to see a professional presentation that day.

There is a big difference between confidence and arrogance. There is a big gap between what is professional and what is not professional. This chapter is about professional appearance.

Unfortunately, too many people have allowed their appearance to be influenced by all sorts of factors, such as habits, culture, "the old days", Hollywood, or their co-workers' sense of style. None of it is acceptable in professional medical sales and I am emphasizing the word "professional".

Presence is about your image when you are talking to a physician or a group of case managers. It is about how you dress and how you carry yourself. A typical physician's depth of perception when it comes to anyone's outward appearance and behavior is much deeper than the one of any other person. Here is why.

Doctors are trained to diagnose and treat diseases and most of them start diagnosing a person before they ask him or her a single question. Whenever a patient walks in, a physician, consciously or subconsciously, begins to diagnose a person, at least initially, based on appearance, quality of movements, and speech patterns.

In "How Doctors Think", Jerome Groopman, M.D. writes about the way one of the doctors was able to correctly diagnose one of his patients by initially reading her body language.

"Everything was a potential clue, telling him something about not only her physical condition but also her emotional state" (Groopman 11).

He then continues:

"The physical examination begins with the first visual impression in the waiting room, and with the tactile feedback gained by shaking a person's hand. Hypotheses about the diagnosis come to a doctor's mind even before a word of the medical history is spoken" (Groopman 12).

Whether you are a sales representative, a baker or a person buying ice cream on the street, you can be sure that a physician looking at you have already given you his preliminary diagnosis. A good friend of mine who happened to be a doctor has admitted to diagnosing everyone she sees, including me.

As a Professional Referral Consultant whenever you are at the doctor's office, you are being diagnosed as well. You may represent the most caring agency in your county and yet the blue tooth in your ear and a Mickey-Mouse tie may subconsciously prompt a physician to diagnose you with a variation of the Munchausen syndrome. Even worse than that, however, is if you are being diagnosed as one of the hundreds of over-the-top sleazy salesmen trying to waste the doctor's time.

Once again, your appearance should be professional and impeccable to the smallest detail. I have put together the rest of this chapter as a collection of appearance points, based on my personal observations of a wide variety of home health representatives.

Dress conservatively, yet with taste.

Nothing in your appearance should be distracting. This means that although it is now common to not wear a tie, retain this accessory because lack of it is, ultimately, distracting (unless you are Ryan Seacrest, of course). Wear matching dark suit, for guys especially. Two tone suit always looks cheap, suggesting that the sales person cannot afford to buy the two matching pieces, in turn, suggesting that he is simply not that good at what he or she does.

Be neat.

When you go to a doctor's office your suit/dress should be impeccably clean, without a wrinkle. Nobody wants to deal with a slob. Nobody. If a sales rep cannot take care of his suit, how in the world is he going to take care of the business that affects people's lives?

Avoid facial hair.

Facial hair of any kind is extremely distracting in sales. Mustache makes a person look older and so does beard. Both are a huge turn off to most of the healthcare professionals and especially the front desk people that cared to share their view of facial hair with me.

This day and age, generally speaking, if you appear way too young or too old, it is hard to be hired for a medical sales job no matter how good your resume is. You may receive a variety of excuses from a potential employer but the real reason is simple. Neither young nor old looks are selling well.

"Four o'clock shadow" for guys on their face may work for all kinds of sales, and may win you some points with the younger teen crowd, but (once again, generally speaking) will not likely work in healthcare sales. Stay away from facial hair as much as possible. Always look neat. Even if you are generally not a neat person, be neat and organized on sales calls.

Keep a neat car.

You never know when the occasion would present itself to give a case manager or a doctor a ride. As unlikely as it sounds, I've done it myself in the past.

Do not be too "out-of-date".

Follow a new trend in conservative wear. Double-breasted suits will kill the sale almost automatically. Another rule of thumb: if you are in doubt on what to wear and what the latest conservative trend is, turn on your local news and boldly copy the anchors' attire. In short, absolutely nothing should distract your target audience from listening to what you have to say. Keep in mind that suits are an investment and may be tax-deductable.

Keep Blue Tooth devices hidden.

Stay away from Blue Tooth while on a sales call. I love my own Blue Tooth and I feel like I cannot live without it sometimes, but during any meeting, I hide it in the depth of my suit pocket. The semantics of a blue tooth is simple – it shows disrespect to your customer and here is why. Blue Tooth symbolizes readiness to answer other people's calls and there can be only one important person during a sales call: that's the one you are talking with.

Say "No" to Chewing Gum.

Trust me, I was not even going to write about it, if I did not observe it in my own experience. Any kind of chewing means disrespect. Every time you chew a gum, think of it as if you were munching on a chicken wing in front of your physician or a case manager, because for them, chewing on anything may signify that you are not willing to give your full attention to him or her. However, do not underestimate the power of a fresh breath (this comes from experience working with sales representatives). *Altoids* may be a good solution to prevent a possible bad breath issue during a sales call.

Say "No" to cell phone.

Silence, as they say in movie theaters, is golden. Turn it off. If it goes off, treat it as an accident and never ever answer it in front of a physician, unless it is in relation to that particular physician's patient.

My Rolex Watch story.

In sales, semantics is everything. Every part of your appearance is a story for a physician. Generally, whenever I go on sales calls with our Professional Referral Consultants, I dress as I preach, very conservatively and not over-the-top, as to not distract my physician's focus from the conversation about our services. One day, however, I made a non-deliberate mistake of wearing a different kind of watch. We had a great luncheon with one of the top surgeons in the city. I was presenting our new services to the physician when his assistant interrupted my speech: "Is that a Rolex watch?" she asked, pointing at my wrist. I said that yes, it was and went on with the presentation only to be interrupted again. This time by the physician: "What model is it?" he asked. "Oh, I don't even know, it's just a gift", I answered, feeling awkward that now the entire room of people was talking about my watch. "Can I see?" a physician asked. "Oh, it's really not as big of a deal as our patient education program," I tried to switch the subject, but to no avail. Two minutes later, the entire room was entertained with comparing my watch with the doctor's. "You sales people, should look money-hungry," Doctor said. "Look at you coming here with their Rolex watches," he said jokingly and yet the conversation was now almost impossible to steer back, leaving us very little time to elaborate on the main purpose of our luncheon – our new service.

That day I've learned an important lesson to pay attention and think ahead even when it comes to the smallest detail. Ever since, I only wear the watch that was given to me by my beautiful wife, Talitha. It is fancy and stylish, and yet not flashy to the point where it will ruin a sales presentation.

NOTES:

_____

_____

_____

_____

_____

_____

_____

_____

_____

Chapter 5

First Dimension: Presentation

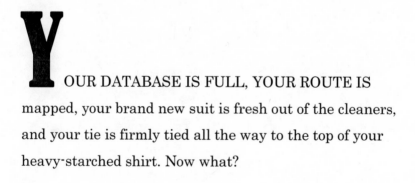

YOUR DATABASE IS FULL, YOUR ROUTE IS mapped, your brand new suit is fresh out of the cleaners, and your tie is firmly tied all the way to the top of your heavy-starched shirt. Now what?

Now it is time to sell, sell, sell! However, I would not recommend jumping into sales at least until you are finished with this book.

Back in the old days of selling, there was no sales cycle. There was only one point-of-sale, one chance to make a great impression, one chance to get the customer, and one chance to make a sale. Today, when selling has become sort of a science from the standpoint of psychology, driven by exceedingly high competition, not a lot of things have really changed. Every time you see your customer (a physician or a case manager in this case), always present yourself as if you only had one chance to make a great impression, one chance to get the customer, and only one chance to make a sale. The only major difference today is that you have a lot less time when talking to a doctor or a case manager: one to two minutes, on average.

You are looking sharp, your smile is on, as you approach a receptionist with your business card to tell them that you were the one that called a few days ago to see a doctor for just a minute. As soon as the receptionist learns that you are not a pharmaceutical representative but, rather, a home health representative, a common response would tend to send you back on the road without even seeing the doctor. The doctor is too busy, there are too many patients etcetera, etcetera.

However, if you have been in sales before, you must remember the old rule of three "No's", and know that it is not your time to leave just yet.

After your first "No", the best thing you can do is to ask if you could see the doctor in-between seeing the patients. If you get another "No", ask if it would make sense to schedule an appointment and try to schedule it on the same day of the week on one of the following weeks, in order to avoid any weekly routing conflicts.

If you are faced with your third "No", confirm the fact that the doctor, indeed, might have a need for a Home Health service and ask to set up a lunch for the office. If you get another "No", there must simply be no need for home health services in this office, and if there is, this kind of situations will be addressed in the later chapter of this book, where we introduce the Sphere of Influence concept.

Before we move on to a different concept of this chapter, it is vital to mention the importance of the reception desk in every doctor's office. On few occasions of my sales experience, I've come to realize that a relationship with the receptionist or an office manager might sometimes be more crucial to my sales than the relationship I have developed with the doctor. I found that in quite a few large and well established offices, the task of giving a referral is actually delegated to someone at the reception, an office manager, a registered nurse or a certified nurse assistant.

In many instances, it may take a few sales calls to find out who, in reality, is in charge of giving home health referrals. This makes maintaining a great relationship with the office staff essential in your marketing efforts. On some occasions, I was able to receive referrals "on the spot" from someone in the office staff, including a receptionist during my regular sales calls. Also, on occasion, even if there is a major disconnect with the physician, I found office people being extremely helpful and resourceful when it came to building a better relationship with the doctor.

ICARE 1.

Whether it is your first, second or twenty-third time at the doctor's or a case manager's office, and whether you are in the beginning or in the middle of your sales cycle, a real

Professional Referral Consultant should always follow a formula that spells out magic:

ICARE 1

- **I**ntroduction

- **C**aptivating attention

- **A**sking questions

- **R**esponding to needs and objections

- **E**stablishing next step of the sales cycle

- Asking for **1** referral

(I)ntroduction.

This part of ICARE 1, in actuality serves two main reasons: to (1) introduce yourself and your company (of course) and to (2) establish credibility in a matter of first 30 seconds to a minute of the conversation with the doctor. And although nobody ever forgets the first reason, almost everyone I've observed forgets the second. Establishing credibility right away is essential in building the foundation for showing a physician that you are a trustworthy company. When awaken at 3 in the morning, a successful Professional Referral Consultant should be able to cite the company-specific credibility statements as if his life depended on it. What are the credibility statements? Only some of the possibilities are listed below:

- How long has the company been in business

- How many locations does the company have

- Who are the company's best, well-established accounts (hospitals or established physicians)

- Awards and 3rd party accreditations

- Any outstanding employment facts

Now let's compare a hypothetical "Hi, my name is Bob Visclosky with Bob Visclosky Home Health" vs. "Hi, my name is Bob Visclosky with Bob Visclosky Home Health. Our agency has been around since 1986 and have 8 branches throughout the United States with 2 branches in the state of Illinois. We are the home health care of choice for the University of Chicago working with cardiologist, Dr.Patel. We have been awarded a Gold Seal of approval by the Joint Commission for 7 straight years in a row. Have you heard about Bob Visclosky Home Health?"

Needless to say, the second introduction will undoubtedly give much more credibility to the person standing in front of the physician.

Now, let's say you do not have a Gold Seal of approval of any kind and you have been around for, maybe just a couple of years. What do you do?

This is when your creativity comes in. Think of the best accounts you have ever worked for as a home health agency. Think of the reputable hospitals your nurses have ever worked for. Think of the hospitals your physical therapists have ever worked for. Think of the specialties of your staff. What if you were to combine all the years of experience of all of the nurses working in your agency, how many years would it add up to? How many skilled nurses and therapists are working in your company?

Be creative and keep it short. Ready? Let's try the credibility statement for a smaller agency.

"Hi, my name is Bob with Bob Visclosky Home Health. We have one of the most experienced nurses in the industry, bringing experience from University of Chicago Hospitals, Lakeshore Community Hospitals and Midwest Surgical with over 100 years of combined nursing experience. We employ nearly 50 skilled nurses on both full-time and part-time basis. Doctor, have you heard about Bob Visclosky Home Health?"

Sound a little better? If it takes you more than 10-15 seconds to spit it out, cut it short leaving only the most important stuff.

(C)aptivating Attention.

Once again, it is just another step in getting a physician's mind off the writing pad and actually listening to what you have to say.

If a doctor had a nickel for every "Our home health offers caring nurses, best physical therapists and experienced occupational therapists, etc." he would have been retired years ago, spending his earnings somewhere in the

Caribbean. There are a few ways to captivate a doctor's attention.

The first one is to present him with a service addition that has not been offered by other agencies. "Doctor, it may be of interest to you that we are one of only 3 home health agencies in the area offering remote monitoring of patients. This system is allowing us to record their vitals even when the skilled nurse is not there. What do you normally do when you have someone that needs extra monitoring after a stroke or any other acute event?"

Or, "Doctor, it may be of interest to you, that we are the first agency in the area with nursing staff that speaks 4 different languages, including Spanish, Korean and Chinese. What do you normally do when you have a patient that requires a nurse that speaks another language?"

Or, "Doctor, it may be of interest to you, that we are the first agency in the area to offer a complete cardiology program for both post-acute and non-acute cardiology patients. What do you normally do when you have a homebound cardiology patient?"

Whether your Home Health agency has only three unique services that are not offered by other agencies or three hundred and thirty three, know them, memorize them, and be ready to recite them in your sleep. Why? Because there was never a day in my experience working with Home Health agency when I was not asked at least a version of "What is so special about your agency? How are you different?" over and over again.

Always, always, be ready to answer the question. In best situations, it will help to establish your credibility. In the worst situations, it will prevent you from being embarrassed. I've been asked that question many times by everyone, from office managers, to nurses, to physicians, to case managers, to people that have no relations to our business whatsoever. Know your differences, use them in your marketing materials and learn to talk about them at all times.

Another way to captivate a doctor's attention is to tie a statistical knot between one of the features your Home Health agency offers and the related data from commonly reliable sources, such as government agencies or statistical data conducted by non-for-profit institutions or associations.

Do a little research, on the internet or from any other source, looking for statistical or fascinating, in any other way, information to capture a physician's attention:

"Doctor, it may be of interest to you that according to American Diabetes Association, one out of three diabetics is unaware that he or she has the disease. It may also be of interest to you that we are the first agency in the area to start a weekly newsletter for our patients that focuses on proper diet, motivation and regular blood sugar checks to diagnose diabetes as soon as possible. What do you normally do when you have a homebound patient who is a borderline diabetic?"

If you fail to establish credibility and captivate doctor's attention within the first 30 seconds of your presentation, you will have the hardest time getting that attention again. The purpose of the Introduction and Captivating Attention is to get a physician to listen. Then what is the purpose of asking a question?

(A)sking questions.

This is probably one of the most important parts of the ICARE 1 because it requires a skill of creating questions that will fulfill three major functions:

- Allowing a conversation to develop

- Letting the doctor/case manager express his/her opinion

- Determine the current needs for home health in the office.

If a physician or a case manager decided to see you, the last thing they want is a commercial-like monologue to take even more time away from their busy schedule. If they are listening to you, that means that there is a chance that they might have a need and a conversation, not a monologue, is the only way to find out what it is.

It may be a basic review for some, however, it is worth repeating over and over: ask open-ended questions! An open-ended question is the one that will trigger another person to respond in a manner, other than a simple "yes" or "no".

"Doctor, do you use home health services in your practice?"
is an example of a closed-ended question that may evoke
nothing but a quick "yep", abruptly ending the dialog.
However, a question such as "Doctor, what do you like
about your existing home health care services" will trigger a
response that will not only get the conversation going, but
will also provide you with a valuable information about the
physician's practice as well.

The second purpose of asking the right questions is to allow
a physician/case manager to express their own opinion on
the subject.

One of the first books I've read at the age of about 11 was
Dale Carnegie's "How to Win Friends and Influence
People." I believe that the fact that I've read the book as a
kid simply in a matter of weeks was probably an indication
that human psychology may have been something I was
born to explore in my lifetime. What stuck with me ever
since, was the fact that a simple, genuine, attentive
listening can help you in both, winning friends and
influencing people. When listening, we, often without
realizing it, let another person know that we are willing to

sacrifice our time for them. We also let them know that whatever their talking about is, indeed, valuable to us. This kind of an interaction, over time, builds trust and friendships.

Thirdly, the reason for asking the right questions is to determine what are the needs of the physician or the case manager when it comes to home health.

Let's say you are competing with one of the largest home health agencies in the region, say, Bigger-S-Better Home Health. A good question may provide an invaluable insight on the next steps of your marketing strategy.

Example 1.

Your question: *Doctor, is there a specific home health you normally use, or is there a preferred list that you try to follow?*

MD's response: *As a part of a physician group, I am "encouraged" to use Bigger-S-Better Home Health, but on cases that require special attention, I use different home health agencies on case-by-case basis.*

Implications: Doctor is not satisfied that he is required to use Bigger-S-Better Home Health and he is, virtually, open to a new, quality Home Health agency as an alternative.

Example 2.

Your question: *What kinds of cases do you normally give to other home health agencies?*

MD's response: *It's an even mix of chronic diseases, from CHF to diabetes. Mostly, though, I give it to the Home Health agencies that bring us lunch (chuckles).*

Implications: Doctor gives his patients to agencies that consistently visit him, opening up new opportunities for small agencies that are persistent in their approach.

Example 3.

Your question: *Doctor, normally, are you the one who makes decisions on what home health agency a referral is going to?*

MD's response: *Only in very specific cases. Most of the time I let my office manager decide. She IS the boss here (chuckles).*

Implications: It may make sense to further talk, or set up a lunch with the office manager to determine how many referrals are normally being handled by him/her.

Example 4.

Your question: *Doctor, percentage-wise, how many of your patients are Medicare patients?*

MD's response: *Hard to say, maybe about one third or so. The rest are either Public Aid or private. We are having a hard time with our public-aid patients getting any type of a home care.*

Implications: It is a good office to continue to visit. Potentially there may be a way to offer some assistance to doctor's Public Aid patients which may need to be discussed with your home health manager.

A few more words about responses. It is important to screen every response through a "motive test". A response can be truthful or not. Throughout the years, I have learned to not take anything at its face value. If a case manager says he does not have any patients to give for home health care right now, it can mean one of two things:

1. They really don't have any patients to give right now

2. They have an established relationship with an existing home health agency and are trying to find an excuse to politely say "No".

If a Doctor tells you that the Office Manager is the one that "really" handles where the referrals go, it can also mean one of two things.

1. The office Manger IS, in fact, the decision maker when it comes to the referrals.

2. The physician already has an established relationship with an existing home health agency and uses his Office Manager as an excuse to politely say "No".

The job of a sales/marketing representative is an all-inclusive job that requires skills of a part-time psychologist, part-time investigator, and, frequently, a part-time food delivery guy. The first two skills, however, are the ones that are of utmost importance. Screen each response for underlying reasons, motives, and things that are being said in-between the lines. Be best at asking, listening, screening and analyzing, so that whatever next step you make or say moves you one step closer to building a valuable and lasting relationship with a physician or a case manager. It is those qualities that will set you apart in the tough world of home health competition.

(R)esponding to needs and objections.

The previous section of this chapter dealt with what we would call quantitative questions, or questions that are intended to focus on the current process of the referral flow. The response to those questions, most of the time, requires a strategic action on the part of the sales representative. This section, however, is going to deal with what we would call qualitative questions. The Professional Referral Consultant's response to the qualitative answers made by a doctor or a case manager normally comes in a form of an additional information presented to him or her in order to educate and advance your sales process. Accurately orchestrated questions about your competition as well as careful response approach can mean a difference between you getting your share of the market and losing your referrals to someone else.

Proactively responding to needs and objections requires top notch presentation, analytical and strategic skills.

This step of the process is so essential in your presentation that we have set aside a place for it to have it's own place later in this book. For now, however, we will skip over to the next step of the ICARE 1 formula.

(E)stablishing the next step of the sales cycle.

Leading The Process factor described in the beginning of this book is about establishing your Home Health agency as a reputable company that follows a set of guidelines and certain processes when it comes to everything, from sales to servicing a patient. At any given point during the sales process, your clients need to know where they stand, what you are, as a Professional Referral Consultant, doing at this moment and what will be your next step.

Unfortunately, if you do not indicate what your next step is going to be for your doctor or case manager, I will assure you, they will decide on your next step themselves. More typically than not, their next step for your sales process will be... not making any steps at all! Out of 10 sales representatives that will stop by the doctor's office, 6 would not even attempt to establish the next step and 3 will forget to do it altogether. Never settle for a physician or a case manager telling you: "Ok, this is some great information. We don't have time for an in-service in the office. I will go ahead and keep the brochure and call you whenever I need you."

No,no and no!

"Dear doctor, please keep the brochure, however as a part of our process, we would like to ask your permission to follow up on our wound care solutions with a 5 minute meeting next week. We promise to be short and to the point. Would that be fair?" Of course it would be.

Become the first class agency in the eyes of a physician by letting them see that you, in fact, follow a process that works like a well-oiled machine. Your potential referral sources will automatically project the experience they had with you as a sales person to the possibility of similar, well-prepared, process-based experience when sending you a referral.

Most of the time, it is essential to be well prepared to tell your clients about their next step in the sales cycle, whether it is a meeting, a lunch, or some kind of product presentation. Even if this is your first day on the job, I recommend using "process" buzzword variations such as:

- Typically

- Normally

- Usually

- As a rule

- As a part of the process

- Normally, when working with other hospitals

- Normally, when working with other physicians

A typical, next-step sentence would sound something like
this:

"If this sounds ok with you, **normally**, we prefer to set up an
in-service or a lunch where we can discuss some of the
benefits of our program in more detail. **Typically, when
working with other hospitals**, we make a presentation for
an entire office. How does next Thursday sound?"

or

"Well, this was a brief overview of what our agency does.
Normally, as a part of the process, we would like to set up a
15-minute meeting where we can actually go into a lot more
detail on other things we do as an a agency. How does next
Thursday sound?"

A couple of words regarding "Next Thursday". No matter
what service you are selling, never, ever, ever give more
than two dates and two times available for an appointment.
Even if your calendar is (and has been for a long time)
squeaky-clean from any obligations or business
engagements.

If you appear as if your calendar is available on any day, it may be misconstrued by your referral source as if you are either a non-effective representative who does not have a lot of business, or a new, not experienced (which means not-credible) representative.

Also, there is that "hurry up, slots are being quickly filled by others" old sales concept that works over and over again, no matter how many times you use it.

On top of that, if you give your referral source too many choices of dates and times, you appear as if you do not have a process that you follow. Moreover, each extra date/time option will cause a doctor or a case manager to spend more time choosing the best meeting time, and, often, may cause them to stall, or back out on a deal altogether.

(1) Asking For One Referral.

There are millions of ways to ask for a referral without appearing to be pushy, but asking for one every time you visit your potential referral source is essential. The number one reason for asking a referral is to get the physician's or a case manager's "wheels" turning. Even if everything they have heard from you during your visit was a typical "blah, blah, blah", whenever you ask for a referral, they begin to think how exactly your service can fit into their practice. Normally, you can ask for a referral by connecting it to one of the features or benefits you have mentioned earlier. If this is your first visit to a doctor's office, it may be a "soft ask" that would sound something like this:

"Doctor, now that you know that our agency has the best diabetes education program in our county, do you know of any of your patients that could benefit from it?"

or

" Doctor, now that you know that our agency has one of the highest Medicare quality rankings, do you know of any of your patients that could use our services?"

The idea is to softly push your referral source into building the mental connection between your agency and his or her patients.

If you will be able to get a referral during your very first visit every time you are at the doctor's office or the hospital, then you have just graduated from the class of Professional Referral Consultants into a class of Miracle Sales Magicians. However, if you are not there just yet, let's focus on further mastering the First Dimension of the sales process.

NOTES:

_____

_____

_____

_____

_____

_____

_____

_____

_____

_____

NOTES:

_____

_____

_____

_____

_____

_____

_____

_____

_____

_____

Chapter 6

First Dimension:

Uncommonly Persuasive

Communication

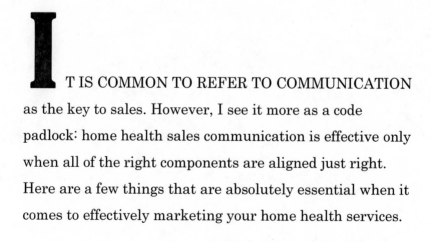

IT IS COMMON TO REFER TO COMMUNICATION as the key to sales. However, I see it more as a code padlock: home health sales communication is effective only when all of the right components are aligned just right. Here are a few things that are absolutely essential when it comes to effectively marketing your home health services.

1.   Use negative motivation to establish a problem. Then solve it!

2. Back up your statements with figures, names and graphs when talking to healthcare professionals.

3. Use feature-benefit approach when talking to doctors or case managers.

4. Use your company's visual sales materials as much as you can.

5. Use metaphors and analogies.

6. Use testimonials.

7. Use common sense when answering questions you don't know the answers to.

Use negative motivation to establish a problem. Then solve it!

It is commonly known that in home health care business, we do not really sell *services*. We sell *solutions* to physician's problems. Figuring out exactly what kind of problems you can solve for a physician is a key step in home health sales. How do we know if a physician or a case manager has a problem that needs to be solved? Most of the time it is done through targeted questions. However, one of the ways to determine or establish a problem that needs to be solved is through the use of negative motivation.

From experience, negative motivation is a much stronger persuasive component than a positive one.

Positive motivation is guided by what your referral *will obtain* by switching to your Home Health agency. Negative motivation, on the contrary, focuses on what your referral *will lose*, if he or she does not switch.

Back in my days of working for a pharmaceutical company, when selling a medication that have proven to reduce stroke occurrences in the elderly, one of the most persuasive statements we would make to a doctor sounded something like this:

*"By keeping your patient on a competitive drug X, according to research, a typical physician **will lose** to death 2 out of every 100 stroke-prone patients as a result of another stroke. This is why most of the neurologists we talk to prefer our drug over drug X. Do you think it is something*

you can use in your practice, doctor? And if yes, do you
have any patients in mind you can put on drug X today?"

Back in my days of selling life insurance, as far back as I
can remember, we never talked about how exciting it is to
have life insurance. All we talked about is how terrible life
is for those who never got one before their loved one died.

Whether it is a life insurance, car insurance or a diet
product, negative motivation is a language of effective sales.
For decades, TV advertisements use the "Are you tired…?"
approach whether it comes to vacuum cleaners or diet pills.
How many times have you seen on TV someone with the
frustrated look on their face, when an announcer asks: "Are
you tired of vacuum cleaners that do not pick up dust?" or
"Are you tired of diet pills that do not work?" The very same
concept worked for decades on TV and it works on most
people in charge of your referrals. Understandably, the
wording needs to be a little different.

Negative motivation, if not used carefully, can occasionally
be viewed as a personal attack or an attack on how your
referral source does business. This is why whenever you are

using negative motivation, refer to *hypothetical* "other physicians" as being the ones who would lose by not using the services of your home health agency. "Other physicians" are the ones that are tired of the lack of quality service when using other home health agencies. "Other physicians" are frustrated with phone calls not being answered when they try to follow up, etcetera. Here we have some of the examples of negative motivators:

Example 1: Multi-lingual staff.

Use of negative motivation to establish a problem:
"Doctor, many of our other physicians have expressed their frustration with trying to find an agency that can provide a bi-lingual nurse within a reasonable timeframe on a consistent basis. Do you find it to be the case in your practice?"

Problem-solving feature:
"Well, doctor, our agency speaks 3 languages other than English: we speak Spanish, Korean and Chinese."

Example 2: Patient Diabetes Education Program

Use of negative motivation to establish a problem:

"Doctor, many physicians we are working with have expressed their frustration with home health agencies that do not spend time with their diabetes patients when it comes to their nutrition, the importance of timely blood sugar measurement, and exercise. They are frustrated seeing elderly patients that think that eating sweet cupcakes is ok, as long as it's not frequent and only a part of a bingo event. At the end of the day, those are the guys that end up in emergency room over and over and over again. Have you had any patients like that in your practice, doctor?"

Problem-solving feature:

"Well, doctor, for about 3 years now, we train and require every nurse to spend extra 10 minutes during each visit to review their current diet and medication compliance, as well as give them encouragement to keep eating healthy even in the company of their family or at bingo events. If a patient is not following the assigned regimen, as a part of our Patient Education Program, he or she is being referred to a Certified Dietician to stay on top of their daily food intake. We give

them diabetes care kit, as well as a free glucose meter if they don't have one. This is why we are yet to have anyone go to the E.R. as a result of skyrocketing glucose levels. Would you like to know a little more about our diabetes education program, doctor?

Back up your statements with figures, names and graphs when talking to healthcare professionals.

The style of communication when speaking to healthcare professionals (specifically, physicians or, sometimes, nurses) is very different from any other communication style. Healthcare professionals are not impressed by abstract language and vague statements. Tell them that your home health agency is the best without backing it up with any data and you may tune them out for the rest of your visit. Tell them that your agency is the most caring without giving any references and you are running the risk of them not listening to another word that is coming from your mouth. Why?

Healthcare professionals, in general, are a unique breed that do not listen to stuff that has no numbers, specific data or a reputable name attached to it. It is not their fault. Years of medical education did that to them and it's great to be a patient of a doctor who is not easily impressed with sales gimmicks. Medical training had taught them to pay attention to **figures, names and graphs**. This is how they've tackled some of the toughest educational challenges and board exams and this is how they tackle everything. Most of the time, at least.

Data is everything. While working for a well-known pharmaceutical company, I had a chance to market a drug that was, to my knowledge merely a sophisticated combination of two very inexpensive drugs available at any pharmacy, priced much less than a buck per pill. Our company combined them into one and manufactured their new pharmaceutical creation with a time-release protective coating. The market price of the new drug was about a thousand-fold of its individual components. How in the world, we were able to sell this new drug to physicians? How in the world, instead of being laughed at, we were able to greatly increase our market share competing with some of the biggest drugs on the market? We used data that turned our simple combination into a state of the art technological advancement. Here is how we did it.

Our company was able to collaborate with an outside institution to conduct a 4-arm study that conclusively proved that the new drug presented a great synergistic effect, which was not observed in any other study. We were able to show our physicians studies, graphs, numbers and figures and dropped off quite a few big names of other doctors and institutions that began to accept the new formulation as the golden standard for patient treatment. We used multi-page visuals and conducted seminars with many physicians present. We had speaker doctors that would talk about our drugs in front of their peers and in front of other medical staff. In short, we spoke the only language that healthcare professionals understand the best: the language of numbers, names and graphs.

Here are some examples of what doctors would listen to and what would fly right over their heads:

Feature that would fly right over healthcare professional's head:	Feature that might catch a physician's attention (figures and names):
Our agency speaks the most languages!	*Our agency speaks **3 languages** other than English: we speak **Spanish, Korean and Chinese.***
We work with some of the major hospitals in the area!	*We are the Home Health Agency of choice working with **Rush North Shore discharge planning** and **University of Chicago's Stroke Unit.***
We are the most caring agency!	***The Director of Case Management at St.John General** has made a comment to his staff that we are the most caring agency.*

We are one of the top Home Health Agencies!	*According to **Medicare.gov**, from June and until now our quality index beats U.S. average on **7 out of 9** parameters related directly to in-home care.*
We are the best when it comes to improvements related to shortness of breath.	*We exceed U.S. average by **19 percent** when it comes to improvements related to shortness of breath.*

Use Feature-Benefit approach when talking to doctors or case managers.

Feature/Benefit approach is a must for any sales representative. Your Home Health agency may be the best agency in the world with the best features among others, however, unless the meaning of those features can be translated into a day-to-day benefit for a physician or a case manager, it is not likely to create a lasting impact. Feature/Benefit approach is a tool that (similar to asking for a referral at the end of each visit) will prompt your potential referral source to start thinking how your service is actually going to fit in his or her practice. The benefit of each feature should be mentioned right after the feature was introduced in a manner similar to this:

Feature that might catch a physician's attention:	Benefit that would prompt a physician to think how your service will fit into his or her practice:
Our agency speaks 3 languages not including English. We speak Spanish, Korean and Chinese.	*… which means that you do not need to waste your valuable time to call 3 different agencies whenever you need a service in a different language. You can only call one. This means your staff will be able to spend more time on working in the office and not on racking up your office phone bills. How does this sound, doctor?*

We are a Home Health Agency of choice working with Rush North Shore. discharge planning and University of Chicago's Stroke Unit.	*… which means that you will never have to second-guess yourself if you picked a credible and reliable agency that deals with the top hospitals in the area. What do you think, doctor?*
The Director of Case Management at St.John General has made a comment to his staff that we are the most caring agency.	*…which means that an independent opinion from a person outside of our agency confirms that we take great care of their patients. Better caring agency can mean heck of a lot less headaches when it comes to dealing with phone calls from patients or their relatives. Do you think this is something that can help your practice on a day-to-day basis, doctor?*
According to Medicare.gov,	*… which means that we*

from June and until now our quality index beats U.S. average on 7 out of 9 parameters related directly to in-home care. The remaining two are in line with both U.S. and state average.	*provide a quality of care that is positively above the national standards on 7 parameters and consistent with national standards on 2 other ones. This way, no one of your patients or department directors will ever be able to question you when it comes to why our agency was your number one choice. This also means less emergency phone calls at night time and many more satisfied patients. How does this sound, doctor?*
We exceed U.S. average by 19 percent when it comes to improvements related to shortness of breath.	*... which means that for every 10 patients you will give us vs. any another agency in the United States, approximately two more will experience a significant*

	improvement when it comes to shortness of breath. This means that for each 100 patients, you will see, potentially 20 less emergencies for you and your staff at night time. That's 20 times less of you waking up in the middle of the night to answer an emergency that did not have to happen. How does this sound, doctor?

As you may have already noticed, each one of the benefit statements start with "which means" and ends with an open-ended question. This kind of a structure should become a second nature for you on your sales calls whenever you bring up one of the features your company offers. As soon as you finish describing a feature, train yourself to say "which means" to jump into the benefit part of your presentation. Always finish with a question that will allow a physician to process the information you have just given him and answer in a way that will cause your agency's benefits to "sink-in" even deeper into the doctor's mind.

Use your company's visual sales materials as much as you can.

Without effective visual marketing sales materials, your agency simply will not be able to compete with the "big dogs" of the business. Everything from business cards to individual sell sheets, to brochures has to be impeccable. Semantics of having impeccable sales materials is somewhat obvious, even if you are not a doctor or a case manager: if your company cannot afford a professionally made brochure, how in the world can it provide a professional quality service? Everything your company presents from a visual standpoint has to be First Class. Period.

In the beginning of year 2008, I had an opportunity to attend one of the legal seminars focused on home health issues. What a nightmare it was to observe agency representatives with homemade, not-evenly cut business cards and brochures that looked as if they just came out of the home printer with its ink about to run out. I know the times for a lot of agencies are tough, but making it so obvious is really not a great idea. This is where it is time to discuss three aspects related to visual sales materials:

- **Types of essential visual materials**
- **Content**
- **Quality**
- **Presentation**

We will start with essential visual materials.

Business cards.

Personally, I recommend having two types of business cards. One kind for a physician and another kind for all of your other types of marketing, including direct-to-patient marketing. Both have to be professionally designed and printed through a printing business.

Here is why I think it is important to have two different types of business cards and why they should be different.

I will begin by saying that I am a firm believer that your business card should say as much about your business as possible. It should list most of your services, all of your contact information and, heck, I even printed a calendar on the back of some of my cards, to lessen the chances of them being tossed away. Some of my cards even had a special appointment lines for a nurse or a visiting physician, just in case if a patient needs one or the other. I also believe that it should be as colorful as possible so that it stands out and is remembered.

However, there is a problem, when it comes to showing information-inundated cards to physicians. The more information you can fit in on one business card and the more colorful you make it, the cheaper it looks in the doctor's eyes, even if it is professionally designed and printed. With the tremendous growth of one-person, self-employed business sales people, the most colorful business cards filled with a variety of information are commonly associated with small, mom and pop types of businesses. The assumption here is this. Large, reputable companies do not need to go down to the level where they need to elaborate on what they do.

Limit your *physician-oriented* business card to your name, title, your logo and contact information printed with the use of only one color. It's better to have a non-glossy (non uv-coated) business card for a simple reason that the physicians and case managers love to write on business cards if they can. For instance, if the doctor likes the fact that your agency speaks Polish language, they will often try to scribble the word "Polish" next to your logo before giving it to their secretary. Our main website has samples of professionally created business cards that are doctor-friendly.

Unlike your physician-oriented business card, your patient-oriented card can be as colorful and as informative as you want to.

Sell sheets.

Small home health agency owners underestimate the use of the sell sheets because they believe that everything of importance is already mentioned in their brochures. I could not disagree more. Typically 8.5x11 inches in size, the sell sheet's role, usually, is to present only one category of products or services your agency provides. Unlike brochures, it elaborates, often in detail, on one of the sides of your agency's services. Presenting an individual sell sheet can be a great reason to stop by the doctor's office one more time, or can be a focus of the entire lunch conversation.

When pharmaceutical companies train their sales representatives, they tend to refer to medical sales as "detailing". The main reason for that is the fact that each visit is used as an opportunity to discuss in more details each and every aspect of a pharmaceutical product. A specific feature and a specific benefit is what makes your product or service unique from a competitor's product or service.

I find that using a variety of discipline-specific sell sheets to capture a physician's attention during the first visit carries a much bigger impact than a brochure. For instance, if your agency prides itself in serving the Spanish community, rehab services for complex orthopedic patients, and a well-developed diabetes-patient education, it is crucial for you, as a Professional Referral Consultant to have a sell sheet for each one of those services individually.

From experience, and especially during a first visit to a doctor, an orthopedic surgeon is often much more impressed by an orthopedic program described in detail on a sell sheet, than by a non-specific brochure that only has one or two bullet points about the subject. Your sales binder should have a good mix of sell sheets for any visit or any possible lunch with a doctor or a case manager. If your agency still does not use sell sheets, ask your manager, or (with your manager's approval, of course) order a set of your own.

Brochures.

Brochures, ideally, should target physicians, case managers, as well as potential patients of your agency. Just like all other visual sales materials, brochures have to be designed and printed professionally to have the maximum impact.

Content of your visuals, whether it is a brochure or a sell sheet, should go hand-in-hand with your verbal presentation. It should establish credibility, captivate attention and present figures, graphs and names to backup your verbal presentation.

Similar to verbal communication, study after study showed that numbers and figures presented in a visual form, in print format, are more easily remembered when used to complement verbal presentation. If you are the one in charge of printing materials at your company, make sure that your data is presented in the form of colorful graphs, bar charts and pie charts with your agency's logo vividly displayed on each and every one of your sales pieces.

Let's imagine a Home Health representative giving a quick presentation to a physician, introducing the following facts without any visuals.

"Doctor, according to Medicare quality index, the percentage of patients who need urgent unplanned medical care is dramatically lower than both U.S. and State Averages." Effective? Maybe.

Now let's imagine the same representative saying the very same thing but this time, he or she will be presenting a physician with a sell sheet that looks something like the one on the following page:

Figure 6.1 Sell Sheet Example

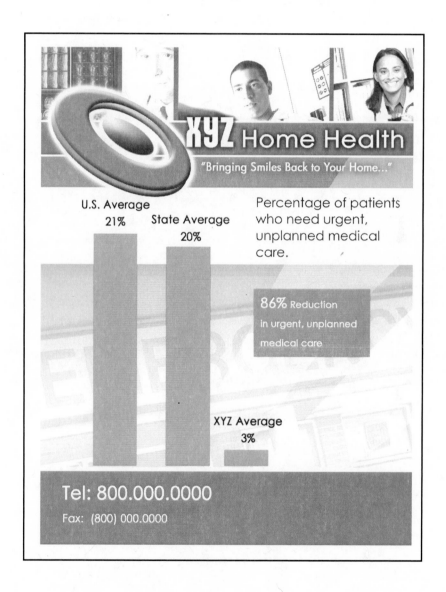

Do you think the physician will remember your data "a little" better by seeing a graphic visual? I guarantee he will.

"Doctor, as you see, the drop in urgent unplanned medical care represents a nearly 86% difference. This means significantly less patients in your practice who will be going to a hospital at night due to diabetic or cardiac events. What do you think about our agency after seeing this data, doctor?"

Verbal statistical statements backed up by a carefully selected visual will have a hundred-fold more impact than verbal statements alone. Period.

Now let's talk about quality. Once again, the basic assumption here is that the quality of your visual materials in the eyes of your potential referral sources is directly associated with the quality of your service.

If your company still does not have a well-established logo, branding, positioning statements, color scheme and a slogan, please feel free to guide your manager to our main website. Visual materials are effective only when they strongly represent all of the above and go hand-in-hand and in concert with your sales cycle and verbal presentation.

As an absolute minimum, your agency should have professionally made business cards, brochures and a set of 8.5x11 sell sheets to support your company's marketing objectives. Everything (with the exception of business cards) should be made in full color on a glossy stock.

Use professional clipart, and do not, I repeat, do not steal clipart from Google or any other search engine. Chances are, if you can steal it from a website, your competition can steal it from the same website as well and (as I have often observed), brochure after brochure of different agencies end up looking virtually the same. If it happens, how would you explain that to your referral sources?

Learning from my own mistakes, I recommend to exclude any of the photographs of the owners, nurses or physical therapists that currently work with your agency. Number one, it looks as if you did not have money to spend on a professional clipart. Number two, if the nurse working for your agency quits, or if he or she, unbeknown to you works for another agency, you may have to re-make the brochure.

Worse yet, your current referral sources may learn that the nurse on your brochure now works with another agency, leading them to think that your company does not know how to keep your staff from leaving you.

If you cannot hire a medical marketing and design company, as a minimum, hire a professional designer with an established portfolio for your brochures. Do not, under any circumstances, let someone do your brochure or sell sheets or any other kinds of visual marketing materials simply because they are a friend of a friend of a friend, even if it is going to cost you nothing because ultimately it will cost you your business.

Although most of the companies do not operate on the level I am about to describe, here is an example of the visual marketing quality that you, as a home health agency representative, are competing with every time you present your brochure to a doctor.

While working with the marketing team of another major medical company years ago (those who are familiar with my resume, know the company I am referring to), I've learned that it took months of market research and questioning of many top physicians and hundreds of potential patients before the very first draft of the marketing material was presented to the company's marketing management team. Hundreds of thousands of dollars were invested into developing a full-blown media marketing strategy and, once again, presented to doctors and patients in exchange for the highly paid feedback... only to conclude that the final version of the marketing blitz was not going to work after all. Months of additional research, hundreds of thousands of additional dollars were invested over and over until a visual aid was developed and introduced into the market to conquer the market share of the company's competitor.

The point here is NOT that you need to spend millions on visual marketing. The point here is that the visuals are highly important and that your top physicians and top referral sources are accustomed to a certain quality of visual presentation. Stay first class! Always have enough visual materials to accommodate an unplanned sales call. Do not let your visuals let you down!

When it comes to presenting your visual support materials, remember the ultimate rule: if you can use them, use them! Bring a full set of your visuals with multiple copies on every single sales call. If you only have two minutes with the doctor, it is much more effective if he or she is looking at the details of your sell sheet, as opposed to any possible deficiencies on your tie or suit. The reality here is this: if you show your visuals to a physician, he WILL look at it for as long as you keep them in front of a doctor.

Keep all the sell sheets in your sales binder. Make your sales binder your Ultimate Referral Consultant Binder! Slide the sell sheets you will be using the most into the top and the back sleeves of your sales binder. Keep the rest of the sell sheets inside, in the protective sheets. Slide a notepad for writing the important stuff in the back of the same binder.

The use of a pen during your presentation is essential. Every time you make a presentation using the visuals, point at the relevant visuals in your binder. Otherwise, as I often found out, some doctors are frequently not quite sure what portion of the sell sheet they need to be looking at.

Use metaphors and analogies.

If a picture is worth a thousand words, then a metaphor is worth a thousand pictures. Carefully chosen metaphors will help you connect with your referral source even more effectively than with just the use of the visuals.

In my experiences, only the highest grade communication professionals, including the best teachers, church leaders and the best physicians are comfortable using metaphors and analogies when it comes to explaining complex subjects to an audience. Metaphors and analogies allow you to break down the benefits of your service to a level easily understandable for all.

However, be careful when using analogies and only use them if you really know what you are doing and only if you have practiced them ahead of time. Write your analogies and metaphors on a separate piece of paper and place them, discretely, in your sales binder.

However, a word of caution. If your analogy is not carefully chosen, or goes outside the "safe zone", instead of one of the most effective tools you can use, it can turn into an unfortunate eyebrow raiser.

Just like it is essential to train yourself to say "which means" after each feature, it is crucial to train yourself in saying "I see it as…" or "The analogy I like to use is…" or "The way I see it, it is kind of like…"

Now we will expand our presentation table to reflect the use of metaphors and analogies. Let's look at some suggested examples on the following pages:

Example 1.

Feature	*Our agency speaks 3 languages other than English: we speak Spanish, Korean and Chinese.*
Benefits	*… which means that you do not need to waste your valuable time calling 3 different agencies whenever you need a service in a different language, you only need to call one. This means your staff will be able to spend*

	more time on working in the office and not on racking up your office phone bills. How does this sound, doctor?
Metaphors/ Analogies	*… The way I see it, doctor, it is kind of like going to one of those buffet places, where you can pick and choose any kind of food you need in one place, as opposed to going from one burger joint to another, trying to find the kind of food everyone in your family would like. We are, in fact, a one-stop shop for your multi-lingual patients. How does that sound, doctor?*

Example 2.

Feature	*According to Medicare.gov, from June and until now our quality index beats U.S. average on 7 out of 9 parameters related directly to in-home care. The remaining two are in line with both U.S. and state average.*
Benefits	*… which means that we provide a quality of*

	care that is positively above the national standards on 7 parameters and consistent with national standards on 2 other ones. This way not one of your patients or department directors will ever be able to question you when it comes to why our agency was your number one choice. This also means less emergency phone calls at night time and many more satisfied patients.
Metaphors/ Analogies	*… the fact that we are in line or better on all of our Medicare OBQI parameters is a big deal for us as a company. The way I see it, doctor, choosing an agency is like boarding a plane. Nobody would trust a life to an airline that is not in line with the U.S. standards.*
	As you can see from this graph, we are not the ones to be intimidated by standards. As a company, we scored so well that doctors that work with us know that we can handle any possible kinds of turbulence when it comes to patient's healthcare. How does that sound, doctor?

Use testimonials.

Whether you are selling a set of fitness DVDs, insurance policy, a pain medication or a home health service to a potential patient or a physician, testimonials are by far one of the most powerful tools available to you as a Professional Referral Consultant.

One of the basic desires of any person is to be able to identify themselves with others in similar situations. We, as people, need to know where we fit or do not fit in by comparing ourselves to others. We need to know whether we can ever become like those other wealthy, healthy and successful folks. Are we standing on the right path to get where we need to be?

About eighty percent of the time, most of the infomercials present testimonials. Majority of the ads are dedicated to showing an average person like you and me using an advertised product or service, while solving his or her needs or fulfilling desires. Home health is no different. Whether you are addressing a physician or a potential home health client, a testimonial is something you cannot ignore in your presentation. I've used testimonials in all of my sales, using and reusing them again and again, until I got my message across. It is hard to imagine anything that sells and convinces others better than testimonials. Here are some of the hypothetical examples.

Example 1:

Feature: Multi-lingual Staff

Supporting Testimonial: *Doctor, one of the physicians we work with is Dr.Patel, who practices on the North side of the city. The office deals with us mostly because of the large Spanish-speaking population in that area and they never knew that our nurses also speak Polish. About a month ago, Dr.Patel was seeing a Polish-speaking lady with severe rheumatoid arthritis and uncontrolled diabetes, in desperate need of home health. Because she was not Spanish-speaking, they have decided to send her an English-speaking nurse from a competitor agency. However, Doctor, as you know, Polish seniors, in general, are not very receptive to English-speaking nurses. Dr.Patel was about to give up on trying to provide her adequate medical attention until he has learned about all the languages we speak as an agency. Ultimately, the patient was re-referred and is currently under our care, as we have nurses that speak*

Polish. Ever since that incident, Dr.Patel told us that we can use them as a reference of the quality multi-lingual service we provide.

Doctor how do you deal with multi-lingual patient situation in your office today?

Example 2:

Feature: Patient Education Newsletter

Supporting testimonial: *Doctor, one of the physicians we work with told us a story about an elderly patient who brought one of our newsletters into his office because it had an article on diabetes screening and she wanted to get one done because of the frequent fatigue and headaches. The patient had borrowed the newsletter from someone who is currently under our care and as a result, she came in to get her blood work done in the office. Luckily, she did not have diabetes, but even if she did, it really could have saved her from all kinds of problems. As a result, although she never ended up needing our services, she was very happy with both, the physician and our company.*

Every single one of our patients gets a newsletter with health related articles, urging them to take better care of themselves and trying to see physician's attention whenever something does not feel right. It is really a win-win for all, the patients, the physician and for us, of course. As of right now, we are the only agency that publishes such a newsletter. What are your thoughts on our program, Doctor?

The more you work in your agency, the more real-life testimonials you will be able to pick up and use for your work as a Professional Referral Consultant. Patient satisfaction surveys that have an open-comment section are another powerful tool which allows you to present your patients' testimonials in a credible manner. If your agency has a policy of keeping this kind of surveys, ask your management if it would be okay to make sections of the surveys allowable by HIPAA laws to be used in your presentations.

Use common sense when answering questions you don't know the answers to.

I've learned from my own experience that what is common sense to some is not necessarily common sense to others. However, whenever you answer questions you don't know the answers to, do not, under any circumstances, make anything up in order to hurry and "make the sale". If you don't know the answer to something, it's ok to say that you don't know the answer, but you will absolutely find out the answer to it by the time you are there next time. Remember that in any given situation, an inexperienced, but honest person is more trustworthy than an experienced liar. As I have learned over and over again, fairness and trust should guide any relationship with your referral source if you want it to last long-term.

Uncommon Persuasive Communication Worksheet.

Uncommon Persuasive Communication Worksheet on the following page is intended for training purposes, as well as the actual sales call preparation. After you list all of the features that separate your agency from others, write down the name of each feature on top of each copy of the worksheet. Take some time filling out the rest of the worksheet according to this section.

Practice presentation verbally in front of the mirror or with a video camera. Often, medical sales training in large companies is not considered complete until the representative's verbal presentation is as good as their conceptual understanding of the sales process. Pharmaceutical companies often have a grading scale for both, knowledge of the product, as well as the verbal adaptation of the company's sales formula. In short, practice, practice, practice.

When practicing, use your company's visuals to back up the statements you make. Get into the habit of supporting all of the details of your presentation with analogies and, most importantly, testimonials from real life examples.

Keep the sheets you worked on in your sales folder, at least until the process becomes second nature in your presentation.

UNCOMMON PERSUASIVE COMMUNICATION WORKSHEET

Feature to be presented	
Negative motivation that can be used to establish a problem	
Describe the feature that can solve the problem, if possible, back it up with figures, names and graphs	
Benefit, or "which means" statement	
Metaphor, analogy, or "the way I see it" statement	
Related testimonial from your experience or the experience of others	
Open ended question	

NOTES:

_____

_____

_____

_____

_____

_____

_____

_____

_____

PART 3

Second Dimension of Home Health Marketing

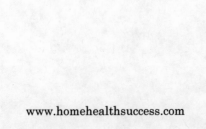

Chapter 7

Second Dimension:

Behind the Scenes of an

Effective Sales Call

WHEN SELLING CLEANING PRODUCTS OR

lawn services, the point-of-sale dimension with impeccable

preparation, presence, and presentation may be all you need

to make a sale. However, no matter how well you are

prepared, no matter how good your presentation is, home

health sales, at a minimum, require a process of effective

follow-ups. In order to give your agency a referral, your

referral source has to, not only know your product, but trust

you, your company and your company's process. This is why

no matter how hard you try, your first visit to a doctor will

always stay only a first step in your attempt to become a

trustworthy Professional Referral Consultant for your

source.

First Dimension of home health marketing process focuses

on Preparation, Presence, and Presentation during your

initial visits to a physician. All of those elements are crucial

in all of the subsequent visits to a doctor or a case manager.

Then, what is the difference between the First and the

Second Dimension?

Second Dimension adds a concept of sales cycle combined

with the analytical and strategic elements. Everything from

Preparation and Presence to Presentation takes on a new meaning and serves a different kind of objectives.

First of all let, us clear up what Second Dimension and Sales Cycle are NOT. It is almost laughable how many sales representatives believe that sales cycle is nothing but weekly or monthly appearance at the doctor's office with the intention to drop off a business card and ask for a referral. Same people show up at the doctor's office over and over again getting nowhere when it comes to getting a referral. Neither the physician nor the receptionist takes those people seriously.

Don't get me wrong, showing up consistently is very important. For your sales cycle to have the most impact, however, each visit has to have a clear goal and purpose in the mind of both, a Professional Referral Consultant and his target referral source. Meaningless pop-ups in the doctor's office will get annoying to the doctor and frustrating for you as a sales person pretty soon.

While it is important to consistently use all of the First Dimension sales tools during each and every sales call, Second Dimension of home health marketing is about focusing on different parts of the sales cycle during the visits. Each will require individual analysis and preparation (preferably written and outlined ahead of time).

As described in the earlier chapter of this book, the Second Dimension is about guiding a sales through 5 major phases: from Initiation, Evaluation, Issue-Specific Presentation, Validation to Service Trial. The entire cycle may take anywhere from 6 to 18 weeks, however, much of it will depend on the type of practice you are targeting.

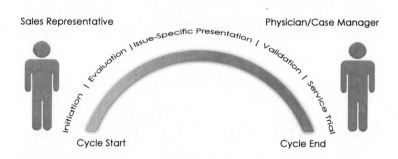

Sales Representative — Initiation | Evaluation | Issue-Specific Presentation | Validation | Service Trial — Physician/Case Manager

Cycle Start   Cycle End

While the goals for each of these phases will be outlined a bit later, it is important to note that in the Second Dimension, "behind the scenes" strategic call evaluation is a crucial step of every sales visit. In Second Dimension, statements made by medical staff are taken apart in order to answer three main questions:

- What did it all mean for us?

- How can we respond to that?

- What is our next strategic move?

Record everything! It doesn't matter if your visit landed you a potential lunch, resulted in an unexpected referral or got you thrown out of the doctor's office: it is your duty to record and analyze everything that happened during each visit

from the perspective of a Professional Referral Consultant.

In Second Dimension home health sales, you are to become

an information sponge. You will be filtering all the

information as it comes in, absorbing what's important and

turning it into a state of the art strategic approach. If your

company has not yet developed a centralized note system,

take time to write down every little detail you have heard

and/or observed at the doctor's or the case manager's office.

The next page shows some of the hypothetical examples of

what can be expected from your notes from each visit and

how it can be utilized for later use.

Visit 1 (Initiation Stage):

```
Physician Name: ********
Address: ********
Phone ********


Visit notes:
First Visit, July 7, 2***


...stopped by doc's office for the first time, spoke
to a receptionist - Jessica - Jessica spoke Spanish
to patients on the phone.

doctor is busy today, but appointment is available
in two weeks when he comes back from Diabetes
conference in New York. Appointment is set for July
20 at 11am.
```

Visit 1 evaluation:

Information (1)	
Receptionist - Jessica	
Analysis	**Strategy**
She may have an insight on doctor's referral flow.	*It may make sense to enter her name into the address book, find out more about her.*

Information (2)

Jessica speaks Spanish

Analysis	Strategy
This office is bilingual.	*It may make sense to present our agency as an agency that has Spanish speaking nurses.*

Information (3)

Doctor is traveling to Diabetes Conference.

Analysis	Strategy
Doctor has an interest in diabetes. Is he going to be there as a participant or a speaker? If he is a speaker, can we use his influence?	*It may be a good idea to present our agency's Diabetes education program. It is important to find out the role he plays in diabetes and how it can be utilized.* *Talking about New York may be a good conversation topic.*

Visit 2 (Initiation Stage):

```
Physician Name: ********
Address: ********
Phone ********
Visit #1

Visit notes:
First Visit, July 7, 2***

Met with the doctor. Told about the company. Doc said
that our educational programs sound really good and he
has not heard of any agencies that can provide it to
their patients on such a high level, however he is not
in charge of where referrals go. All of his home
health patients come mostly from the hospital. All of
them are referred by the hospital's discharge planners
and they already have 3 different agencies that they
use all the time, depending on what part of the county
the patient lives in.
```

Visit 2 evaluation

Information (1)	
Doctor is not in charge of the referrals.	
Analysis	**Strategy**
Although he is not in charge of the referrals, doctor's opinion still matters when talking to discharge planners who are.	*Meet with the discharge planners.*

Information (2)

Education programs strike a chord with the doctor.

Analysis	Strategy
Educational programs apparently are important for his patients and this may make an impact on discharge planners.	*When meeting with discharge planners, it will be vital to bring up the importantce of educational programs to the doctor.*

Information (3)

Discharge planners already use 3 different agencies, depending on what part of the county the patient lives in.

Analysis	Strategy
*Hospitals have patients in different parts of the county and we have the capability to serve **all** of them.*	*We have to emphasize to discharge planners the fact that our agency serves **all** parts of the county.*

Each note should be well recorded and turned into a part of

a strategic puzzle piece of the overall sales cycle, leading

you confidently from one stage to the next. The next chapter

will focus on the best way to organize each stage of the sales

process.

NOTES:

_____

_____

_____

_____

_____

_____

_____

_____

_____

_____

_____

_____

Chapter 8

Second Dimension:

The Five Stage Difference

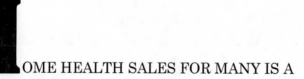

H

OME HEALTH SALES FOR MANY IS A
difficult concept and it is understandable, mainly because it
does not fit our typical view of sales. First of all, unlike any
other type of sales, home health service does not have a
price tag attached to it. Secondly, all of the typical selling
points of a home health agency are seemingly intended to
benefit not the doctor or the case manager, but a vague
third party. Thirdly, there is no contract where a doctor or a
case manager signs in order to start using your services.

Instead, they can "kinda" decide whether to use your services or not whenever they want. The problem here is this: if a sales person does not view his or her task as a well-structured sale, neither does his or her potential referral source. The Second Dimension of home health marketing is here to fix that.

We will begin with a brief overview of the five-stage process.

As we have already mentioned in this book, Second Dimension of home health marketing consists of five stages: Initiation, Evaluation, Issue-Specific Presentation, Validation and Service Trial. It is important to mentally separate the stages, since each one has a different goal and purpose, although often they do, in fact, overlap. It is just as important that the potential referral source sees your visits as a well-structured process, not just a meaningless office pop-up.

Initiation. Typically, the goal of initiation is simple: to contact the office of a doctor or a case manager and figure out whether it would make sense to continue the sales process. If this is your first visit to the office, use your basic, well-prepared ICARE1 techniques described earlier in this book. Remember, however, to keep your very first visit short and sweet. I never expect my first sales call to last for more than 2 minutes. It should be more than enough to present a sort of an ICARE "teaser" to a physician or a case manager in order to set up an in-service where you will be able to go over your agency's services in much more detail. Typically, you have 2 minutes to introduce yourself as a credible agency, captivate attention, ask and receive a response to at least a couple of questions, establish the next step and "soft-ask" for a referral that could benefit from your home health agency. Establishing the next step here is essential and a relatively simple process. By showing a physician and/or a case manager how much your home health agency is unique and different from others, it is only natural to ask him or her to schedule a lunch or a more extensive meeting at a later date. That first official sales appointment is where you will make your first transition from Initiation to Evaluation.

Evaluation. The goal of Evaluation is to present a detailed overview of the company's unique services in a luncheon or other professional setting, while laying a foundation for

what is probably the turning stage of our sales cycle –
Issue-Specific Presentation (by getting to know your
contacts and investigating their real needs).

The first luncheon or the first official sales appointment is
where the transfer from Initiation to Evaluation happens.
Since lunch allows for more time (typically 30 minutes to 1
hour) to present your services and ask questions, ICARE1
should take up your entire presentation.

Know the IC in ICARE1! Countless times I've faced
situations when case managers would come up to the lunch
room, one by one, politely pick up a brochure, look me
directly in the eyes and ask, "So tell me how is your agency
better than what we have been using?" The worst answer is
"we provide nurses to Medicare patients as well as
everything you can see in our brochure." Blah-blah-blah! If
you don't use your IC, the only memory left in the case
manager's mind after the lunch would be a peppery,
rotisserie chicken aftertaste. Your brochure will be thrown
out and your company forgotten.

If several case managers come into the room at different times, I use a 30-second version of Introduction + Captivating Attention presentation over and over while giving the case managers a fresh pack of marketing materials, making sure that everyone else in the room hears me repeat my presentation. The best outcome in this stage of an appointment is when one of the case managers takes it upon him/herself to start presenting the benefits of your agency to other case managers who walk in a little later than the others. This is when I like to jokingly tell my sales reps that "our job here is officially done!"

This, of course, is ridiculously far from reality.

Remember ICARE1! Right after an impressive (I+C) presentation, the rest of the lunch (A+R) should be dedicated to strategic questions focused on establishing the needs and the current issues of the physician(s), the case manager(s), or the medical office. The list of strategic questions should be prepared ahead of time to make the appointment as productive as possible. Take names of the attending staff and detailed notes as they will soon be the basis in your next stage – Issue-Specific Presentation.

When asking questions, whether it is about an existing home health referral workflow or an existing relationship with a home health agency, learn to separate junk from facts. It is important to assume that the office already works with at least one preferred home health agency. The reality is, most of them work with at least two. Keep that in mind when filtering the answers you will be getting from either a doctor or a case manager. When analyzing their answers, keep their motivation in mind. Chances are, before they will be willing to share with you any of their needs or home health related issues, their initial motivation will probably be to protect the existing relationship. Below is an example of learning to separate junk from facts and finding the way to cross-examine some of the answers.

Question and Answer:

- *Doctor, do you have a specific workflow when it comes to referrals? How do you choose which agency to use?*
- *Oh, we have a list of about 50 agencies that do an in-service for us and we rotate them down the list.*

Assumption:

Doctors, typically, already have an established relationship with at least two home health agencies and it is unlikely they would give referrals to ALL of the agencies that do an in-service for them. This means that more questions may be needed.

Cross-Examination Questions and Answers:

- *Doctor, what if one agency is superior in wound care and a patient has a severe wound situation, is it still your policy to go down the list?*
- *Oh, no, we have an agency that does an outstanding wound care for us.*
- *So, in extreme cases, you pick your agencies based on their specialty?*
- *You could say that.*
- *What are the specialties that are of utmost importance in your practice?*
- *We deal with a high volume of orthopedic patients and it is important for us to have an agency that provides us with consistent results.*
- *Does your current agency provide you with consistent results?*

- *Somewhat. They have been pretty good in the beginning... Nowadays, however, they have been really slacking off. I think they begin to take our referrals for granted.*

This conversation is a typical example of how a physician's answer can completely change during the course of an appointment. Each dialogue should be guided by a carefully selected set of questions and an assumption that he or she already has an existing relationship with at least one home health agency. In the example above, we were not only able to start "defogging" their referral flow, but also identified a need for a consistent service, which, their current agency cannot provide.

The end of the appointment should be a brief summary of the appointment and, of course, (E) establishing the next step of the sales cycle (Issue-Specific Presentation) and asking for at least 1 patient that could use the services outlined during the appointment. Each case manager and physician should be given a business card and marketing set you have prepared earlier.

From Evaluation to Issue-Specific Presentation

Issue-Specific Presentation should be your next major luncheon or appointment after the Evaluation luncheons/appointments. Issue-Specific Presentation is the time when your audience begins to look at you as a consultant, as opposed to an average sales representative.

No matter how good of an ICARE1 presentation you made during the evaluation phase of the sales cycle, it is only a step in the process, not the sale itself. Between the time of your first ICARE1 presentation and your Issue-Specific Presentation appointment is the time to gather as much information as possible to learn what are the real needs and motivation of doctors and/or case managers you gave a presentation to. Some pieces of this puzzle can be uncovered during your first lunch appointment. However, more often than not, you will have to gather the rest of the information during your follow-up visits. A lot of the useful information can be uncovered by talking to the staff of the medical office or the hospital floor.

I remember one time when I have scheduled a big lunch with the doctor only to find out that he could not attend it due to an emergency. I decided to go on with the lunch anyway. This lunch, unlike my prior meetings with the doctor, turned out to be the most valuable experience ever. I've learned more about the doctor, his relationship with other home health care agencies, and the motivation behind his referrals than I could ever learn during my regular visits. "Doctors working here are really something," one of the office assistants told me. "For the last several years, they have only used two agencies. However, they still allow other agencies come in and feed the staff, keeping their hopes high." That was interesting, I thought. "The only way to get through to a doctor is by talking to his wife, who is the general manager here," she said. "Don't tell anyone I told you this," she added. Needless to say this has completely changed my view and my strategic approach when it came to marketing in that office.

Unexpected information like that can pop seemingly out of nowhere and it is better if it appears sooner than later.

This is why I recommend to make several office visits before the big Issue-Specific Presentation luncheon or an appointment. The reason for it is two-fold: to build a rapport with the office staff and the case manager or the doctor, and to make sure that most of the puzzle pieces of the doctor's real needs/motivations are put together in time for the Issue-Specific Presentation.

Each one of those pre-visits should follow a basic ICARE1 formula with a little more emphasis placed on the A (Asking Questions) part of it. By listening and by building a clear picture of your customer's needs and your agency's solutions, the Issue-Specific Presentation will seem to be a natural and necessary step in your potential referral source's mind, as opposed to just another meaningless sales event.

Issue-Specific presentation should be done in a professional setting with all of the key staff member and physicians present. The IC in ICARE1 this time should be very brief. After about a minute of introductions and captivating attention, it is important to let the attendees know that in-spite of all the great things your agency has to offer, this meeting will not be about you, it will be about them.

The Captivating Attention phase of ICARE1 should be turned into an effective presentation summarizing the unanswered needs of the medical office. All the major points you have ever uncovered during your Evaluation phase should be brought up and addressed, one by one, in front of the staff. The better prepared you are, the better the outcome of your presentation will be.

After you asked all the questions and responded to all of the objections, it is time to summarize the result of the meeting and establish the next step – Validation, a separate phase where a specific referral guideline will be given to the staff members. Why is an entirely separate step necessary?

Well it isn't. However, if your goal is to get as many referrals for your efforts as possible, then I suggest you make it a separate stage in your sales process.

Validation

By conducting an Issue-Specific Presentation, you make a move that shows a doctor or a case manager that you have listened to what they had to say. It is your way to show the office that you are ready to step into the consultative shoes of a Professional Referral Consultant. Validation step is where your referral source, with your help, creates a plan to commit to your services.

Unlike most sales, in home health marketing, there is no proverbial dotted line to sign. There are no contracts, no obligations, and once you leave the office, the doctor or the case manager are still free to use whoever they desire.

Validation step, in some ways, intends to replace written commitment with the psychological one. This step is necessary in order for a doctor or a case manager to firmly establish in her and/or her staff's mind that from this point on, their office will be using your home health agency and reaffirm the type of patients that will be referred to your company. Validation step consists of implementation discussion, implementation plan, as well as, implementation date.

At the time when I used to work in laboratory sales for one of the companies in Chicago, I started using validation step 100% of the time without any exceptions. This would virtually guarantee that the next time a medical office would need a laboratory, they would use us as agreed on, starting at a specific date. Here is how it worked.

A little background first. Normally, collection of laboratory specimens in the medical office requires the use of supplies and a centrifuge to spin blood before storing. It also requires standard requisition forms and lockboxes for after-hour pickups. All of those things come standard and are readily available in most of the medical offices I dealt with. After the Issue-Specific Presentation, however, I would always sit down with the office manager separately, to talk about the office's transition to begin the use of our services (the validation phase).

My job was to tell the office manager that if they would like to work with our laboratory, it is important to set a date for us to come in, train their staff, and replace all of their laboratory-related supplies with ours. From that point on, we will be providing them with our own supplies and equipment. When an office manager would ask why do we need this, I would tell them that it was a matter of our company policy to prevent any mistakes related to lack of training and malfunctioning equipment. During the meeting, we would brainstorm on the best ways this training can be done and the communication workflow after the implementation. The implementation date was the date after which the office would always begin to use our services.

The idea behind the replacement of their supplies and equipment and providing additional staff training was a graceful psychological transition of the office from the use of the competitor's lab to the use of ours.

The reality is, many of the competitive laboratories back then did not care enough to go an extra mile and spend their resources on equipment, supplies and training. After all, all of the laboratory equipment and supplies are the same everywhere and so is training. Why bother?

The lack of validation step in our competitor's marketing gave us an advantage and, of course, many accounts to follow.

Now, what about validation step in home health marketing?

Skipping the validation step is the biggest mistake a home health salesperson can make. Most of the sales calls I've ever observed, end with great presentation and a hope for the best. Hoping for the best is not a part of the Second Dimension. Your referral source should make a mental transition to being committed to your home health care.

The following are the steps that are necessary for such a transition after your Issue-Specific presentation:

Set an implementation date. Get the case manager, office manager or a physician to commit to a date when implementation will occur. Explain that on that date you will make a Validation in-service in order to provide medical staff with the customized referral workflow.

Let everyone in the medical office know about the implementation in-service. Make sure that everyone in the medical office knows about the implementation and the in-service that will take place.

Customize your referral materials. Customize everything from your patient letters to your referral forms to have the physician's name, address and phone number on it. The patient's welcome package can have the physician's name on it. Have it done professionally, if possible.

Conduct an implementation meeting or an in-service on the scheduled date.

The entire staff of the physician's office or the case management unit should know that, although any patient in their office will always have an ultimate say in choosing of their home care treatment, after several meetings, you would like to give everyone official welcome packages made specifically for their office and your home health agency. Explain how to use forms and what kinds of patients will benefit from using your agency's services. Thank everyone for their time and express your confidence in a successful working relationship.

This is going to be the point at which the Validation stage will be complete and Service-Trial stage will begin.

Service-Trial Stage.

This stage of the cycle is mostly a matter of common sense. If you are like most of us, you don't buy your clothing without trying it on, neither do you buy a car without taking it for a "spin" at least once. Therefore, although the doctor may have verbally and mentally committed to use you and only you, all of your efforts are going to go down the drain if the doctor or the case manager has a bad customer experience once they give you their first referral.

In my own experience, if you really mess up a referral, you may get your referral source to give you only one more chance if you can convince the physician or the case manager that it was only an exception. However, if you mess up twice, your chances of getting another referral are equal to about zero, in spite of continuous visits, lunches, perfect presentations etcetera, etcetera. A successful Service-Trial stage will set you up for a successful transition into the Third Dimension of home health marketing. Failure at this stage should not be an option.

As a Professional Referral Consultant, it will be your job to follow your Service-Trial referral through so that there is no miscommunication or misunderstanding.

Isn't it the job of the medical department of my agency? Of course it is. However, remember, that the medical department for the most part, could care less if it is your first referral or your last one. Majority of the medical staff at your agency are salary-based and losing a referral will never affect them (at least in the short run) as much as it will affect you and your job. Always follow through on your Service-Trial referral so that it does not end up to be your last one!

NOTES:

_____

_____

_____

_____

_____

_____

_____

_____

_____

_____

PART 4

Third Dimension of Home Health Marketing

Chapter 9

Third Dimension:
Sales Oxygenation Concept

YOU HAVE JUST RECEIVED YOUR FIRST referral and followed through with it. A physician is thrilled with your services and you cannot contain your excitement because you have worked hard on this account applying the process described in this book. Everything worked out just fine, both a discharge planner and a physician made a mental transition and have promised to use your services. Shouldn't it be enough to guarantee a flow of continuous referrals?

It will be, if you utilize the main secret to continuous referrals: Sales Oxygenation concept.

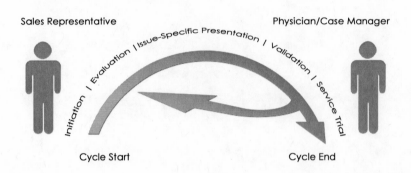

Just like our brain cannot function without blood being constantly oxygenated at the lungs, your referral flow will stop if it does not follow a similar kind of process. In the Sales Oxygenation process, Evaluation stage serves as the lungs for your referral flow.

Once again, it is not enough to simply drop by and show your face even after you have already received your referral. The Sales Oxygenation process requires somewhat less strategy, but just as much effort on your part.

Sales Oxygenation is all about going back to the Evaluation stage of the cycle even though you have already received a referral from a physician or a case manager.

Follow up. If you ever see someone on the street appearing to talk to someone on the phone while saying something that sounds like "Five….Ok….Five…Hm…Five…Five…Five…Yeah…Five", it is not because their crazy. Most likely, they are talking to Gallup organization, answering to service follow-up questions with customers. This company's job is to ask random customers to rate the service they have just received on a scale of one to five, five being the best. Why do companies care? Because they know that if at the Service-Trial stage they will get the lowest score of one and do not correct the situation right away, the customer simply will never come back to use them again.

After the Service-Trial stage, follow up immediately! Stop by and thank them for the referral. Explain to the physician or the case manager what's going on with the referral and if everything is going according to plan so far. Most of the larger medical centers are sick and tired of spending their time and efforts on the phone trying to find out whatever happened to the referral they have just given to an agency. This is why they tend to stick with the ones that have a great follow up system in place.

Get Feedback. Get detailed feedback on your services from an office employee who is NOT your main referral source. Here is why. If something went wrong with your first referral, you should learn about it and fix it before you talk about it with the one who made the decision to choose your agency.

Present new information. Stop by the office to let them know that your agency keeps up to date with the latest in the industry. Present new stuff, whether it is a new service that your agency offers, a new brochure, a new sales sheet, a new patient package, a new newsletter, a service that allows the physician to submit their referrals over the internet, or anything else that can help your agency to maintain an image of a company that stays on top of things.

Evaluate the needs. Yes, you may have already evaluated the needs of the medical office only a few weeks ago. Now it is time to do it again. Follow the process described in the previous chapter, ask questions and address any issues immediately.

Issue-Specific Presentation and Validation. Once an issue or a need for a new service comes up, proceed to Issue-Specific Presentation stage and have an in-service on how a new change will benefit the medical office. Do not skip validation stage! Set the implementation date for the new changes to make sure that everyone on the staff knows what is to come. Each one of those things will enable you to establish yourself as a Professional Referral Consultant, whose job is to not just sell a physician's office more services, but rather help them establish themselves as a first-class medical office or institution.

NOTES:

Chapter 10

Third Dimension:

Power Strategy Charts

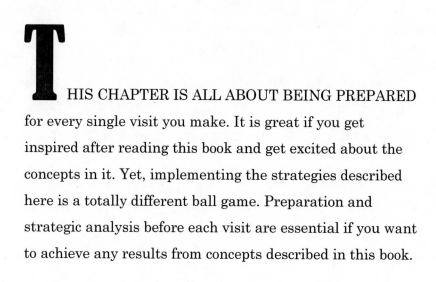

THIS CHAPTER IS ALL ABOUT BEING PREPARED for every single visit you make. It is great if you get inspired after reading this book and get excited about the concepts in it. Yet, implementing the strategies described here is a totally different ball game. Preparation and strategic analysis before each visit are essential if you want to achieve any results from concepts described in this book.

I am a firm believer in anything that has to do with computer databases. However, I also believe that certain things should be left to paper. I highly recommend that you get a few 3-ring binders to keep track of your accounts before entering the data into your computer database (I consider each person who has a potential to give you a referral as a separate account).

Each binder should contain a set of Power-Folders containing information about each one of your accounts located in a specific geographic location, be it a hospital, a medical building or a zip code. This way if you give an in-service or a lunch in a hospital with 12 case managers where 7 of them have promised or can potentially give you business, each one of those 7 should have a Power-Folder in your binder.

Each one of your Power-Folders will contain, what I refer to as Power Strategy Charts (the compilation of guide-sheets that will help you structure your sales process).

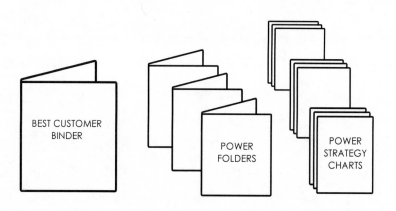

The first reason to start using Power-Folders is to zero-in on the individual needs of each one of your accounts. Remember that each one has a different need and motivation when it comes to referrals.

The second reason is to make an impression on your potential referral source. By having a folder with their name on it, you are not only flattering them, but also telling them that you are taking what you do seriously. It is important to remember that most of the high-volume referral sources see dozens of sales people every day. They realize that most of them care only about their business. This is why personalizing your approach when it comes to each account is essential.

I label each one of my binders "Best Customer Binder", just in case your account asks you about it, or if you accidentally leave it at the doctor's office after making a sales call. Never write anything negative such as *"July 8: It is the second time I meet with Dr.Knowitall, but he just doesn't get it. I will have to bring more cookies next time."* Always write with the assumption that one day, accidentally, your referral source may read its content. The downloadable version of the Power Strategy Charts can be found on our website as an additional resource.

The next pages show examples of the strategy charts. The bold fill-in boxes on those charts represent information that should be prepared PRIOR to making a sales call. The rest of the boxes are to be filled in during or after the sales call is made, in order to effectively evaluate the situation. Each table consists of ICARE1 fill-in boxes, as well as boxes that are intended to be used for your follow ups. This will allow you to be on top of your accounts at any given time.

Initiation Stage

MEDICAL OFFICE NAME	
LAST NAME/TITLE	
FIRST NAME	
PHONE NUMBER	
ADDRESS	

OTHER INFO:

Tip: Write down Doctor's likes or dislikes as well as interests here. You can also use this field to write down office hours info.

Presentation (60-120 seconds)	Response
I	
C	*Tip: Prepare your target-specific presentation and questions and write them here.*
A	
R	*Tip: Write down Doctor's/Case Manager's responses here.*
E	
1	

Date of follow-up visit	Goal of follow-up visit	Overall result	Date of Next Visit

Evaluation Stage (In-Service)	

Introduction/Captivation (5-20 minutes)	Response
I	
C *Tip: Prepare and write down key points for your Introduction/Captivating Attention*	

Ask /Respond (20-40 minutes)	
A 1. 2. 3. 4. 5.	*Tip: Prepare and write down specific questions for your potential referral source here.*
R 1. 2. 3. 4. 5.	*Tip: Write down Doctor's/Case Manager's responses, top needs and motivations here.*

Establish Next Step/Ask for 1 Referral (1-3min)	
E	
1	

Date of follow-up visit	Goal of follow-up visit	Overall result	Date of Next Visit

In-service sign-up sheet

#	Name	Position	Notes

Issue-Specific Presentation		
Introduction/Captivation (5-10 min)		Response
I		
C		

Issue-Specific Presentation (20-30 min)	
Issues	Solutions

Ask /Respond (10-20 minutes)
A
R Response

Establish Next Step/Ask for 1 Referral (1-3min)			
E			
1			
Date of follow-up visit	Goal of follow-up visit	Overall result	Date of Next Visit

In-service sign-up sheet

#	Name	Position	Notes

Validation Stage

IMPLEMENTATION DATE/TIME _____

#	Implementation Task	Assigned to	Notes

Tip: Use this sheet to write down what implementation tasks have to be done, who will be in charge and when they should go into effect.

Service Trial> Sales Oxygenation™

Date of follow-up visit	Goal of follow-up visit (feedback, new information, evaluation, issue-specific presentation or an in-service)	Outcome	Next Visit Date

NOTES:

_____

_____

_____

_____

_____

_____

_____

_____

_____

_____

PART 5

Fourth Dimension of Home Health Marketing

Chapter 11

Fourth Dimension:

Spheres of Influence

SPHERE OF INFLUENCE CONCEPT IS
probably the most advanced and the most effective
approach in sales today. From experience, in order to work
best, it will require a great deal of teamwork. However, I
believe that it can be achieved via individual effort as well.
Sphere of Influence is where pharmaceutical and large
medical companies invest millions in. The result of the
successful approach of the Sphere of Influence concept can
increase your healthcare sales immeasurably. Often, it

requires a great deal of effort and a great deal of commitment. However, the successful outcome will outweigh any investment and will save the company money on other types of less effective marketing.

The Sphere of Influence approach is based on the observation that individual doctors, case managers, as well as medical institutions, have their own professional influences. These influences often overpower their demand for your product or service. Frequently, you can try to sell to a physician the best thing since sliced bread only to face a wall of "thank-you-but-no-thank-you". On the surface, everything you do appears right and yet your target medical office, for a reason unknown to you, keeps referring patients to your competitor.

Although no doctors think alike, their medical decisions often are affected by a number of those influencing factors. Most of the major ones belong to one of the following categories:

- Patient's Well-Being
- Structural Influence
- Relationship-Based Influence
- Regulatory Influence
- Financial Influence
- Personal Interest Influence

Patient's Well-Being Influence is the one that influences medical decisions based on the doctor's belief of what is best for the patient. In the ideal world, the patient's well-being should be the primary influencing factor for the doctor and yet, both me and my wife had a misfortune of knowing doctors for whom the patient's well-being is so far down the list, that it is questionable why they got into medicine in the first place. Our agency has long made a choice to only work with physicians, whose main influence is the patient's well-being, with all the other influences being either parallel or secondary to it.

Structural Influence is the one that influences a lot of physicians' medical decisions due to the written or unwritten rules established either by the individual medical institution or by the medical community in general.

An example of those "influencers" is described in detail in the next chapter, "Structure-Based Sphere of Influence".

Relationship-Based Influence is the one that influences a doctor's medical decision as a result of respect for an opinion of a more senior physician or an "opinion leader" in a certain specialty within a medical community. More on that is in the chapter "Relationship-Based Sphere of Influence."

Regulatory Influence has an ability to influence a doctor's medical decision as a result of government regulations and if not followed, may jeopardize the physician's license or turn into a lawsuit.

Financial Influence is the one that influences a lot of physicians' medical decisions based on a wide variety of financial factors, from third-party reimbursements, to situations where a physician is a part-owner or a direct financial beneficiary of a certain enterprise.

Personal Interest Influence affects a doctor's medical decision if he or she has a strong personal interest (medical, or otherwise) outside of his practice. An example can be an involvement in medical research, charitable program or a sport.

How are these important in home health sales?

First of all, most of the home health sales I have observed are conducted in a manner that implies that there is no secondary motivation when it comes to a doctor's decision. However, it is no secret that many of the medical decisions made by a doctor are guided by things such as the type of insurance a patient has, his relationship with other doctors, medical networks and hospitals, etc. Each decision a doctor makes is a result of a combination of many such influences. If you, as a Professional Referral Consultant, do not take them into consideration, your effectiveness diminishes significantly.

Second, knowing a doctor's influence factors will allow you to affect the other, seemingly unrelated aspects of his or her practice in order to stimulate the referral flow.

Knowing your doctor's or his staff's influence factors can be the difference between small and large-scale marketing success.

For instance, if you are using only a *Patient's Well-Being* message during your sales visit to a doctor for whom one of the main decision influences is *Financial Motivation*, chances are, your message would fall on deaf ears, unless you somehow add a *Financial Motivation* message to your sales approach as well and vice versa. If you are using a *Financial Motivation* message on a doctor, whose main decision factor is *Relationship-Based Influence*, you will have a hard time figuring out why your physician keeps using the agency recommended to him by his senior physician, who is also his mentor.

This chapter was written to establish the importance of understanding the many factors that can influence a physician's decision. The next chapter will focus on some of the real-life examples of how a strategic use of these influences can dramatically increase your sales.

In this book, we will primarily focus on two types of influence spheres: Structural and Relationship-based. Working for large medical/pharmaceutical companies gave me a chance to observe and participate in both. As a result, I am going to give you a few examples that allowed me to learn a great deal about the Sphere of Influence concept in real life situations.

NOTES:

_____

_____

_____

_____

_____

_____

_____

_____

_____

Chapter 12

Fourth Dimension:

Structural Sphere of Influence

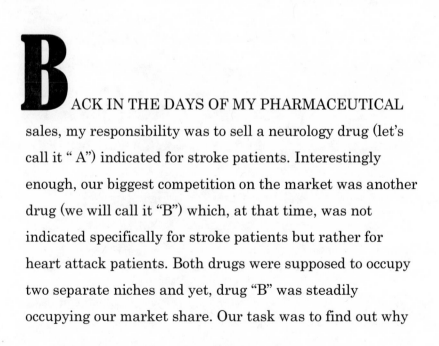

BACK IN THE DAYS OF MY PHARMACEUTICAL
sales, my responsibility was to sell a neurology drug (let's
call it " A") indicated for stroke patients. Interestingly
enough, our biggest competition on the market was another
drug (we will call it "B") which, at that time, was not
indicated specifically for stroke patients but rather for
heart attack patients. Both drugs were supposed to occupy
two separate niches and yet, drug "B" was steadily
occupying our market share. Our task was to find out why

we do not have a solid market presence in places where we should have a virtual monopoly.

One of the biggest prescribers of Drug B, our competitor, was the nicest, very well-known primary care physician (and my friend), who we will call Dr.Great. Step by step, we were following our sales cycle, explaining the features and the benefits of Drug A. We explained that there was no competition to our drug and it really helps to save people's lives. We brought in a number of great lunches with home-like food for the staff of 15 and the best sushi in town for the doctor. Deep down, I was not too concerned if Dr.Great ever prescribed Drug A, as I considered our friendship above any prescriptions he has ever written. We've had conversations, at length, about trials for our drug as well as other methods of preventing secondary strokes in patients. Dr.Great is the kind of doctor, for whom the Patient's Well-Being always comes first. This was why I was confident that he would make the best decision for his patients no matter what. We were impressed that Dr.Great finally agreed to give out our samples and to write prescriptions for Drug A. We were ecstatic! Dr.Great was one of the biggest prescribers in the region, and it gave us confidence to have the backing of one of the best doctors in our community.

As a part of the marketing process, pharmaceutical companies have data of all the prescriptions ever filled by pharmacies on a week-by-week basis, sorted by each doctor. To our disappointment, when the script data came in, we've learned that Dr.Great's prescriptions of Drug A were not great at all. Neither did we see any results from other primary care physicians. We could not understand what was going on and have decided to schedule another lunch to find out.

"I really like your drug", Dr. Great told us. "I like it's features and its benefits and I see how it could benefit my patients. However, most of my stroke patients come from the neurologist (let's call him Dr.Mind) down the street and a big neurology group on Broadway and I don't feel it is right for me to switch the prescriptions of a specialty doctor."

We were shocked, but glad that we were able to pinpoint the issue. The situation appeared to emerge as a classic example of Structural Influence, which was affecting Dr.Great's primary concern of the Patients' Well-Being. Although physicians can prescribe pretty much anything they want in spite of what any neurologist recommends, the unwritten rule dictates that if a specialist recommends Drug B, then the primary care physician will tend to stick with that recommendation.

We knew exactly what to do. During a follow up meeting that day, I drew a diagram that was a pen-drawn version of this:

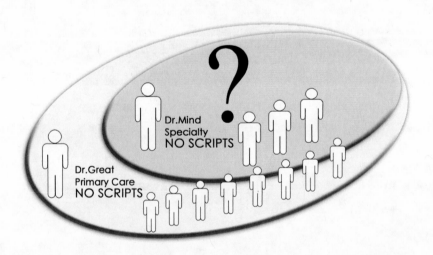

We have set up an in-service with Dr.Mind and followed our sales cycle process to discuss the benefits of Drug A for stroke patients with the neurology group nearby. Dr.Mind warmly welcomed our team and has agreed that Drug A is the best drug out there. He agreed to prescribe it, and so did the other specialty doctors from the neurology group and yet, the most we saw was a couple of scripts here and there. Frustrated, but not defeated, we have, once again, talked to each one of the neurologists, individually, to find out what's going on.

"I really believe in Drug A and its benefits" each one of the doctors said. "However 90% of the patients that we see come from the ER, where all of them are given Drug B and we cannot educate the entire hospital staff on what to write. We deal with dozens of stroke patients every week and we are simply as frustrated as you are when it comes to switching every single patient to Drug A without patients questioning it every time."

Now that the ER of the local community hospital came into picture, everyone on our team felt like we were part of some Agatha Christie novel, chasing an invisible someone who was suffocating our team's efforts. We met again to discuss what we had to work with that day. Once again, we had a doctor who believed in the benefit of our drug for the Patients' Well-Being, but the unwritten rule of his practice prevented him from switching all of the stroke patients on Drug A due to the Structural Influence coming from the ER.

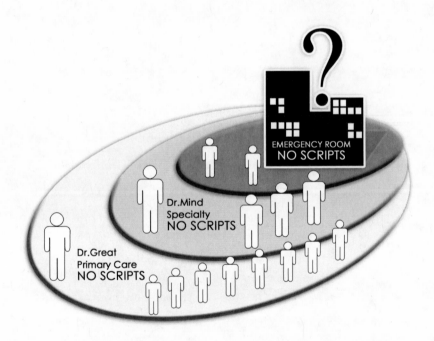

Another month passed by before we had a chance to do an

in-service in the community hospital's ER. With multiple nurses and doctors popping in and out, we have explained to them that Drug A is the only one indicated for stroke patients and Drug B should be used mostly for heart attack patients. We have printed out a Prescription Information packet and everyone in the ER have admitted that they have never realized that we were the only drug indicated for stroke patients whereas Drug B has never carried such indication. However, they said, their hands were tied because they were merely following a hospital-established protocol for their stroke patients. If we could change the protocol, they said, they would gladly put all the stroke patients on Drug A.

For us, it meant that without changing an ER protocol, we will not see prescriptions for any of our stroke patients. We found out that all of the hospital protocols were put together by a committee consisting of specialty physicians, including one cardiologist (we will call him Dr.Heart) who happened to be the one writing the ER protocol for stroke patients and who was a fan of Drug B because this was also a drug that he prescribed for his heart attack patients. Apparently, the sales representatives for Drug B were clever enough to convince Dr.Heart to use the same drug for stroke patients due to similarities of characteristics, in spite of the fact that B was not yet approved by FDA for strokes.

Once again, tired and weary, we have decided to put our efforts into Dr.Heart's office located in the hospital itself. But how do you influence a guy who is one of the most respected doctors to change an opinion about a protocol? We have sponsored one meeting after another before trying to get his "OK" to the ER protocol changes. After all, how can a hospital use a protocol established by a cardiologist for its neurology stroke patients?

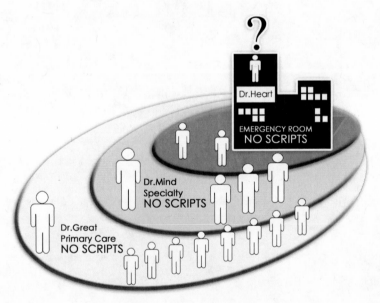

Long story short, before I left the company, the protocol was on schedule to be changed. All of the stroke patients arriving at the community hospital were to follow a protocol that required them to be placed on Drug A and a recommendation to follow up with the neurologist. All of the neurologists were to continue prescribing our drug for the duration of the rehab process. As a result, ALL of the primary care physicians were to prescribe Drug A as a main medication for stroke patients. This meant that Dr.Great, as well as the majority of the other primary care physicians in the area, were to start the use of Drug A. This was a text book example of Structural Sphere of Influence Concept.

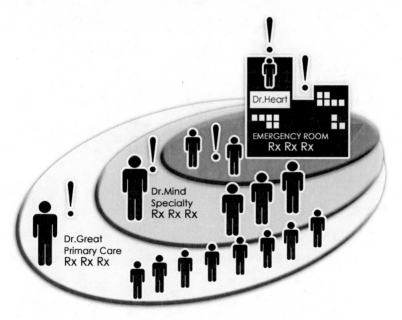

The Sphere of Influence approach is, in many ways, similar to the approach the detectives investigating a crime. It takes a good dose of strategic questioning, diplomacy and perseverance. Once all of the pieces of the puzzle are in place and the sphere of influence map is drawn, the results are not only self-gratifying, but financially rewarding as well.

When it comes to home health marketing, decoding Structural Spheres of Influence are imperative to successful sales. Home health agencies that do not understand this concept will eventually be pushed out of the big marketing picture.

In one example, after a number of attempts to prove ourselves to a well-known surgery center, we were able to come to an agreement to be an exclusive agency serving the post-acute patients right after they attend a several day rehab center of their choice. The unwritten rule states that a referral made by a surgeon following a post-acute event has to be followed by other doctors until recovery, in spite of the fact that they were treated by another agency prior to hospitalization. In turn, Relationship-Based Influences dictate that once a surgeon or a specialist takes over a patient's treatment, no primary care doctor can intervene in the midst of the rehabilitation process and switch them to another agency. Although it took a lot of effort on our part as well as on the part of the well-respected surgeon and his assistant to emphasize the exclusivity of their preference of our home health agency when it came to referrals, it ended up to be a win-win for all, the doctor, the patient and, of course, for our agency as well.

Structural Sphere of Influence is a very powerful form of marketing when it comes to increasing your referrals (as long as you can back it up with quality service) and can fill a whole book by itself, however for now we will move on to another type of marketing approach, Relationship-Based Sphere of Influence.

NOTES:

_____

_____

_____

_____

_____

_____

_____

_____

_____

_____

Chapter 13

Fourth Dimension: Relationship-Based and Other Spheres of Influence

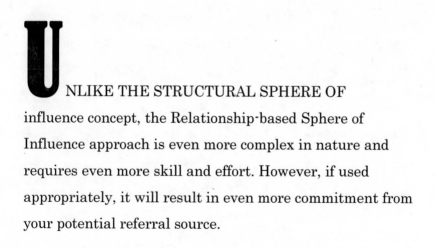

UNLIKE THE STRUCTURAL SPHERE OF
influence concept, the Relationship-based Sphere of
Influence approach is even more complex in nature and
requires even more skill and effort. However, if used
appropriately, it will result in even more commitment from
your potential referral source.

A great lesson of the Relationship-based Sphere of
Influence approach was the one I received while working for

a pharmaceutical company while developing a brand new marketing area for Drug A, competing with Drug B.

Unlike my first example, our "target" physician was, in fact, a neurology specialist (we will call him Dr.Neuro) working with a group of other neurologists, high-volume prescribing physicians, none of which used our company's Drug A. All gave complete preference to Drug B for their stroke patients.

Remember the two minute average sales call rule? Well, this guy would not let us say anything beyond "Hello, Doctor, how are you doing?" It was a miracle to even get him to look at a sales rep from our company.

Talking to the neurology group's office manager, we figured that the best approach to talk to anyone on the staff was to set up a breakfast for all 25 staff people, and this is exactly what we did. We spent extra time and effort to make sure that we ordered our breakfast from the best, out of town place, known for its best homemade pancakes and an outstanding food selection. We showed up early to make sure that everything goes as smooth as possible. And it did.

With the exception of one small detail: Dr.Neuro never showed up for breakfast.

While talking to the other doctors, later, we found out that Dr.Neuro was spending most of his time at a different, out of town hospital where he shared an office space with one of his colleagues who was a graduate from the same school as Dr.Neuro. We were also able to find out that Dr.Neuro remained a close friend with his medical school professor, let's call him Dr.Harvard.

Dr.Harvard, although semi-retired, was always invited to oversee some of the more complex procedures performed by Dr.Neuro. We have discovered that if Dr.Neuro would ever listen to anyone's opinion, it would only be the one of Dr.Harvard's.

This meant that all of our company's efforts from that point and on were focused on Dr.Harvard, in spite of the fact that he was no longer seeing patients, was not writing scripts, and only had a consultant position at the hospital.

As Dr.Harvard refused to meet with anyone without being paid, our company has invited him to "consult" us regarding our marketing materials and strategies. While "consulting" us, doctor was genuinely impressed with our drug's mode of action and benefits. Being a highly influential physician, he was also a prime candidate to be recruited to be one of the lead physicians in the ongoing efficacy trials for Drug A, a position he gladly accepted. As a consultant, he also agreed to have a heart-to-heart talk with Dr.Neuro and his team of doctors regarding Drug A and its importance when it came to stroke patients. We provided the lunch and Dr.Harvard did all the talking for us. Needless to say, this was a turning point for both Dr.Neuro's prescribing habits, as well as for our sales numbers.

Relationship-based Sphere of Influence approach is probably one of the more effective approaches out there. Many of the well-respected physicians are very well familiar with the sales game, yet game or not, an opinion of someone they highly respect carries a weight that no competition can withstand.

Other Spheres of Influence. Of course, some spheres of influence are not the ones you would want to get into. One of the Spheres of Influence to absolutely stay away from is the financial one. Whenever a medical center, a physician or a case manager is expected to benefit financially in some way from a home health agency they are using, it will be nearly impossible to introduce your home health agency's benefits and features, which always is a losing situation for a patient.

One thing, though, will always stay true. Your best referrals and your most consistent referrals will always come in abundance from sources where the primary motivation is the patient's well-being. Medical offices and hospitals where *patient is always number one* are easy to spot and will be the most beneficial for you and your agency. The patients love them, the employees love them, and whenever the priorities of your home health agency are the same, you are going to love doing business with them too.

NOTES:

_____

_____

_____

_____

_____

_____

_____

_____

_____

_____

Notes and Resources

Some of the quotes used in this book were taken from "How Doctors Think", written by Jerome Groopman, MD (Mariner Books, 1st Edition). Those interested in understanding how physicians make decisions may find it very informative.

Additional helpful resources may be found on www.homehealthsuccess.com. This site was created specifically to aid readers of this book and is being updated regularly.

Please visit www.nahhcp.org to learn more about National Association of Home Health Care Providers. This organization was created to unite home health agencies into a strong political and legal voice, advocating for protection of care providers and their patients when it comes to responding to the increased pressure coming from insurance companies, adequate reimbursements and service coverage. In addition, NAHHCP is designed as a resource to help individual owners to make steps in saving costs while improving quality of care, as well as protecting agencies from unethical business practices.